30 Days to Living a God Life not Just a Good Life

Walking in God's Ways

One STEP at a Time

{GROUP STUDY}

SHAUNA J. WALLACE

Published in the United States of America.
Published November 2016.

Shauna Wallace

BECOMING WHOLLY HIS

shaunawallace.com
Twitter: @ShaunaJWallace
Instagram: @shaunajwallace
Pinterest: pinterest.com/ShaunaJWallace
Facebook: facebook.com/OfficialShaunaJWallace

Table of Contents

Introduction 5

How to use this study 11

Week 1 – Belonging to Jesus & what He wants of His family 15

   LESSON ONE 16

   Day 1: Let love be without hypocrisy 18

   Day 2: Abhor what is evil 22

   Day 3: Cling to what is good 26

   Day 4: Be kindly affectionate to one another with brotherly love 30

   Day 5: In honor giving preference to one another 36

Week 2 – The inside job: heart attitudes & the who of our hope 43

   LESSON TWO 44

   Day 6: Not lagging in diligence 46

   Day 7: Fervent in spirit 51

   Day 8: Serving the Lord 56

   Day 9: Rejoicing in hope 61

   Day 10: Patient in tribulation 66

   Day 11: Continuing steadfast in prayer 71

Week 3 – The outward expression of the inside job: how we treat others 77

   LESSON THREE 78

   Day 12: Distributing to the needs of the saints 80

   Day 13: Given to hospitality 84

   Day 14: Bless those who persecute you 89

   Day 15: Bless and do not curse 93

   Day 16: Rejoice with those who rejoice 98

   Day 17: And weep with those who weep 104

Week 4 – Midsets 109

   LESSON FOUR 110

   Day 18: Be of the same mind toward one another 112

   Day 19: Do not set your mind on high things 117

   Day 20: But associate with the humble 123

   Day 21: Do not be wise in your own opinion 128

Week 5 – Trusting God & letting Him be God 135

   LESSON FIVE 136

   Day 22: Repay no one evil for evil 138

   Day 23: Have regard for good things in the sight of all men 144

   Day 24: If it is possible, as much as depends on you,
      live peaceably with all men 150

   Day 25: Beloved, do not avenge yourselves 157

   Day 26: But rather give place to wrath; for it is written,
      "Vengeance is Mine, I will repay," says the Lord 161

Week 6 – The good that overcomes evil 167

   LESSON SIX 168

   Day 27: Therefore, "If your enemy is hungry, feed him;
      if he is thirsty, give him a drink 170

   Day 28: For in so doing you will heap coals of fire on his head 174

   Day 29: Do not be overcome by evil 180

   Day 30: But overcome evil with good 185

Week 7 – The Potter & His perfection 193

   LESSON SEVEN 194

Conclusion 197

Let's connect! 199

Appendix A: The One Way of Salvation 200

Appendix B: How to Find Something in the Bible 206

Appendix C: Answer Key 209

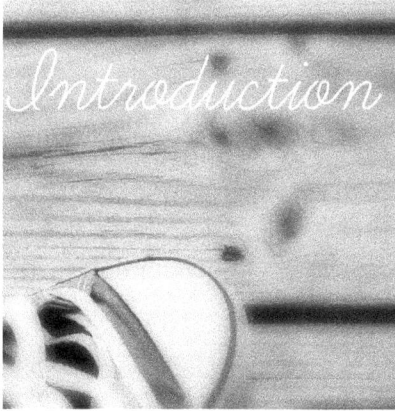

This hybrid devotional Bible study and application journal was born out of failure. If you ask me my number one priority as a parent, I will tell you it's teaching my children to know God, to recognize Him at work around them, to know His word and to walk in a love relationship with Jesus. Not just now, but when they no longer live under our roof and must decide to follow Jesus because it's what *they* want to do, not just because it's all they've ever heard us tell them. This requires intentional instruction of the sit-down-and-teach kind, as well as the talk-about-it-as-you-go kind, "speaking of them (God's commandments) when you sit in your house, when you walk by the way, when you lie down, and when you rise up" (Deuteronomy 11:19, parentheses added for clarification).

Sounds impressive, right? But if you watched my actions, you would see me commit my time to all kinds of other good and worthy activities that distract me and drain the minutes of my days, superseding one of the most worthy uses of my time. You'd find me busy doing good things, but not the God things I know the Lord specifically presses me to do.

The Bible calls it sin: "Therefore, to him who knows to do good and does not do it, to him it is sin" (James 4:17). In my life, this happens when my conviction is curtailed by my own corruption. The inconsistencies in my talk about Jesus and my walk make me feel like a fraud writing about living for Him and knowing the fullness of what He desires for us. I doubt myself and lose my confidence.

When I confessed my lack of discipline and my unwillingness to obey to the Lord and asked Him what to do, He answered. One morning in the time I set aside for Bible study, I encountered Romans 12:9-21 in a book on motherhood. I happened to be copying passages in my journal for easy reference as I noted what God was showing me, and when I turned to the passage in my Bible, the subhead jumped off the page: *Behave Like a Christian.*

Instead of copying the passage in paragraph form, I randomly decided to copy it one tenet at a time, and then I counted them and found thirty. The wheels started turning. Thirty life apps we can utilize every day in our walk with Christ. What if I took each one, learned what the Bible teaches about walking it out, and then taught it to my children? It would be a great tool for intentional discipleship!

And so *30 Days to Living a God Life not Just a Good Life: Walking in God's Ways One STEP at a Time* began as a way to practice what I preach, one step at a time. I want to love Jesus by the way I live, not just the way I talk. Through action, not just intention, the way 2 John 1:6 describes: "This is love, that we walk according to His commandments. This is the commandment, that as you have heard from the beginning, you should walk in it."

I want to walk the path of life (Psalm 16:11) in the big stuff and the little stuff. Consistently. When it's hard. When I'm tired. When I'm worn down and burned out. When the world presses me to do the opposite and the burden is heavier than I can handle. When Satan makes the path of destruction look so attractive and I'm tired of saying "No" all the time. When little compromises seem harmless, but lure me and my family off the path of life.

What about you? Or your kids? Do you want to walk out or deepen your relationship with Jesus but don't know how? Do you need someone to mentor you, but right now, no one is? Are you discipling someone and looking for a way to intentionally instruct them in the way they should go? Is your Sunday school, Bible study or small group looking for a practical study that will help you live your faith in your everyday life? I pray each of these thirty days brings fresh understanding and inspiration for doing what Jesus wants us to do.

Authenticity: It's All About the Walk

Hypocrisy destroys our witness of Jesus. It destroys our children's faith. It destroys relationships with each other. It is hurting the church. It is hurting people desperate for Jesus and unwilling to turn to Him because of what they've observed of many who proclaim to be His followers, who say one thing and do another. We may tell our kids to "Do as I say, not as I do," but actions speak louder than words.

Why worry about how we walk? We're not talking about the literal physical steps we take with our legs and feet, but rather the way we move through life one decision at a time. The way we conduct ourselves, make our way and make use of opportunities.

To walk in God's ways is the evidence of abiding in Jesus: "He who says he abides in Him ought himself also to walk just as He walked" (1 John 2:6). Paul says in Colossians 2:6-7, "As you therefore have received Christ Jesus the Lord, so walk in Him, rooted and built up in Him and established in the faith, as you have been taught, abounding in it with thanksgiving."

Jesus says:

> I am the light of the world. He who follows Me shall not walk in darkness, but have the light of life (John 8:12).

> A little while longer the light is with you. Walk while you have the light, lest darkness overtake you; he who walks in darkness does not know where he is going. While you have the light, believe in the light, that you may become sons of light (John 12:35-36).

Paul talks about walking in the light in Ephesians 5:8-10: "For you were once darkness, but now you are light in the Lord. Walk as children of light (for the fruit of the Spirit is in all goodness, righteousness, and truth), finding out what is acceptable to the Lord."

A little further in that same chapter, Paul talks about walking in wisdom: "See then that you walk circumspectly, not as fools but as wise, redeeming the time, because the days are evil. Therefore do not be unwise, but understand what the will of the Lord is" (Ephesians 5:15-17).

When we put our faith in Jesus, we are "buried with Him through baptism into death, that just as Christ was raised from the dead by the glory of the Father, even so we also should walk in newness of life" (Romans 6:4).

To walk in this newness of life, we must "put off, concerning your former conduct, the old man which grows corrupt according to the deceitful lusts, and be renewed in the spirit of your mind, and that you put on the new man which was created according to God, in true righteousness and holiness" (Ephesians 4:22-24).

We must learn to walk the talk, "by faith, not by sight" (2 Corinthians 5:7), not just because it's important for us, but also for others. It is how we become a light to those in darkness.

Behave Like a Christian

So how exactly do we live a God life by walking in His ways? When you write out Romans 12:9-21 by each of the Christian virtues Paul lists, here's how it breaks down into thirty principles or life apps:

1. Let love be without hypocrisy.
2. Abhor what is evil.
3. Cling to what is good.
4. Be kindly affectionate to one another with brotherly love,
5. In honor giving preference to one another;
6. Not lagging in diligence,
7. Fervent in spirit,
8. Serving the Lord.
9. Rejoicing in hope,
10. Patient in tribulation,
11. Continuing steadfastly in prayer;
12. Distributing to the needs of the saints,
13. Given to hospitality.
14. Bless those who persecute you,
15. Bless and do not curse.
16. Rejoice with those who rejoice,
17. And weep with those who weep.
18. Be of the same mind toward one another.
19. Do not set your mind on high things,
20. But associate with the humble.
21. Do not be wise in your own opinion.
22. Repay no one evil for evil.
23. Have regard for good things in the sight of all men.
24. If it is possible, as much as depends on you, live peaceably with all men.
25. Beloved, do not avenge yourselves,
26. But rather give place to wrath; for it is written, "Vengeance is Mine, I will repay," says the Lord.
27. Therefore, "If your enemy is hungry, feed him; if he is thirsty, give him a drink;
28. For in so doing you will heap coals of fire on his head."
29. Do not be overcome by evil,
30. But overcome evil with good.

This is the walk. It's not a checklist to earn salvation. It's not about being good in our own effort or power. We can't. It's not so that we can perform better for Jesus. It's not so our efforts can gain the attention of God or others. It's not to make us feel better about ourselves so we can have healthier self-esteem. It's simply to learn what it looks like to walk on the path of life and experience the abundant life Jesus came to give (John 10:10).

Learning to Walk

As babies, we learn to walk one step at a time. The same is true in our walk with Jesus. We learn one S.T.E.P. at a time:

Scripture
Teaching
Example
Practice/Prayer

That is what we'll do together this next thirty days (and it's totally okay if it takes longer; see *How to Use this Study*). We'll look at one life app at a time, memorize it and see what else the Bible has to say about it. We'll look at examples of what it looks like, and then we'll put it into practice.

A few housekeeping items. I do not assume to know what version of the Bible is best. The scriptures I quote or reference are from the New King James Version unless otherwise noted. When asked to answer a question based on a scripture, our answers may vary based on the different syntax between versions. Not to worry! Do your best, or use a free mobile or online Bible resource, like *Olive Tree* or *www.blueletterbible.org*, which allows you to search any scripture in any version.

Each day, you'll have the opportunity to answer some questions for reflection and application. You will get out what you put in, so I encourage you to take the time to let God's truth sink in to a place where it begins to rule your thoughts and choices. If you're anything like me and it stresses you out if you don't know whether or not you arrived at the correct answer, *Appendix C* has the answer key. Check away!

One final thing I want to stress. This walk must be done in love, "as Christ also has loved us and given Himself for us, an offering and a sacrifice to God for a sweet-smelling aroma" (Ephesians 5:2). This should humble us; it should not produce pride or judgment of others, which stink.

People are watching what we do, so let's heed Paul's counsel: "Walk in wisdom toward those who are outside, redeeming the time. Let your speech always be with grace, seasoned with salt, that you may know how you ought to answer each one" (Colossians 4:5-6).

As we embark on this walk together, I pray that we "may walk worthy of the Lord, fully pleasing Him, being fruitful in every good work and increasing in the knowledge of God; strengthened with all might, according to His glorious power, for all patience and longsuffering with joy; giving thanks to the Father who has qualified us to be partakers of the inheritance of the saints in the light" (Colossians 1:10-12).

The Very First Step

The first step in our walk with Jesus is responding to His gift of grace by faith. If God doesn't give us eyes to see and understanding to receive, none of this will make any sense. We do not have the ability to live this way on our own because it's in direct opposition to our selfish nature. He must first and foremost turn our hearts to Jesus and our desires to walking in His ways. Only then can we love Him enough to follow His path of life and intentionally take each step according to His instruction.

Is the Lord turning your heart to Him? Have you responded in faith? Please don't take another step in this study before turning to *Appendix A* and learning more about *The One Way of Salvation*.

Well, it's time for our first S.T.E.P.! Let's begin by praying Ephesians 3:14-21 for ourselves and each other, that we may "walk in the way of goodness, and keep to the paths of righteousness" (Proverbs 2:20).

Let's Pray: For this reason I bow my knees to the Father of our Lord Jesus Christ, from whom the whole family in heaven and earth is named, that He would grant you, according to the riches of His glory, to be strengthened with might through His Spirit in the inner man, that Christ may dwell in your hearts through faith; that you, being rooted and grounded in love, may be able to comprehend with all the saints what is the width and length and depth and height – to know the love of Christ which passes knowledge; that you may be filled with all the fullness of God. Now to Him who is able to do exceedingly abundantly above all that we ask or think, according to the power that works in us, to Him be glory in the church by Christ Jesus to all generations, forever and ever. Amen.

Your thirty days may be literal and consecutive, five or six at a time, or sporadic as you can get to them. You could even tackle one a week for thirty weeks and spend six days practicing that one life app. One of my daughters divided each day into two, focusing on the *Scripture* and *Teaching* one day and the *Example* and *Practice & Prayer* the next. You might work through this study on your own, allowing each teaching to disciple you, or you might complete it with a small group or even your family. There is no right or wrong way; just make it work for you.

If you are studying *30 Days to Living a God Life not Just a Good Life: Walking in God's Ways One STEP at a Time* in a small group and have someone to teach the live lessons, each participant will want to have a copy of the *Group Study* book, which includes fill-in-the-blank lesson guides. (If you are interested in teaching the live lessons and need facilitator materials, please contact me at shaunajw@yahoo.com.) If you are not going to have live lessons or are working through the study on your own, use the book for *Individual Study*.

Regardless of whether you go through the study alone or with a group, you'll find the thirty life apps grouped into six weeks, each with a theme as follows:

Week	Homework	Focus
Week One	Days 1-5	Belonging to Jesus and what He wants of His family
Week Two	Days 6-11	The inside job – heart attitudes and the Who of our hope
Week Three	Days 12-17	The outward expression of the inside job – how we treat others
Week Four	Days 18-21	Mindsets
Week Five	Days 22-26	Trusting God and letting Him be God
Week Six	Days 27-30	The good that overcomes evil

If you are using the *Group Study* with live lessons, you will also have a Week Seven with a concluding lesson on *The Potter and His Perfection*.

Make-Up Work

Life happens, and you might get behind or miss a few days. That's okay! Just pick it back up and keep going. If you're participating in a group, pick up where they're at so you can stay current in your group's discussion time, and then as you have time, go back and complete what you missed. While each life app is presented in the same order as they appear in our passage, they can be studied independently.

There is no perfect way to complete this study! If you hate filling in blanks and journaling, then just read the lessons and the scriptures. If you've never done a Bible study before and find you don't know exactly what to do, just do what you can and keep coming back. You will learn!

I will say, and this will come as no surprise: the more you put in, the more you'll get out, so put in as much as you can!

Reflect & Review

Each week closes with *Reflect & Review*, an opportunity to look back and summarize what God has taught or shown you that week. I encourage you to take the time to flip through your notes and pull out the key truths that jumped off the page or struck close to home. As I did this, God solidified some of the most powerful lessons He taught me as I went through this study myself. (Not only did He spend two years teaching me as I wrote the study, but every time I had the opportunity to share with a group, I cracked open a fresh copy of my own and did the study right alongside them. I'm pretty sure I'm the one who needed this study the most!)

You can also use this section to make note of any exercises you didn't get to finish or want to repeat.

What You'll Need

As you work through *30 Days to Living a God Life not Just a Good Life: Walking in God's Ways One STEP at a Time* here are a few things you'll want to have in addition to your book:

1. A pen, pencil and/or highlighters,
2. A Bible, and
3. 3x5 cards for scripture memory (the goal is to memorize the entire passage).

Group Study

As you see in your *Group Study* book, your first week is an introduction and overview, followed by your first week's assigned work at home. Each following week, the first part of your group session will be spent discussing the previous week's homework, followed by a brief teaching to introduce the next week's focus. The final week includes discussion and a concluding lesson.

Behind the title page for each week, you'll find a fill-in-the-blank handout for that week's live lesson, followed by the homework for the coming week. Depending on the size of your group, level of participation and time available, you may want to select only a few of the discussion questions while skipping others. If participation is low, you can use the discussion questions as a guide for highlighting the main points from the previous week's lessons. If this happens, give priority to reading the scriptures that are referenced out loud together, and then answer the questions from the text as a group. The most important words are the words that bring eternal life, so spend your time on God's words, not mine.

Family Study

Depending on the structure of your family, the number, ages and stages of your kids and your family's commitments and rhythm, your study is likely to be very unique to you. It was actually my desire to create a resource parents could use to disciple children of any quantity or age that inspired this study. When you have more than one child and they are in different stages of development, it can be hard to faithfully engage in formal Bible study with each one. I personally never succeeded at this! I desperately wanted something that would apply to all my kids no matter their age or stage.

When working through the study as a family, you can use either the *Group Study* or *Individual Study* book, depending on whether or not you want to teach the live lessons.

Here are some ways to adapt this study to your family:

- Approach it like a small group study using the available resources. Be sure to have the *Group Study* book and facilitator materials if you choose this format. Parents and older kids can complete an agreed upon amount of work on their own during the week and then get together for discussion and that week's lesson.

- Use it as a daily, weekly or monthly family devotion, memorizing each day's scripture together, reading the *Teaching* and *Example* sections out loud and then answering the questions together as a group.

- Modify the work to your family and your kids' ages and walk with Jesus. Feel free to assign certain verses to certain people and share the load of looking them up and recording the answers. If there are a lot of scriptures to look up, just do a few. There are no hard and fast rules and there is certainly no condemnation. Make it work for you!

- Tackle *Practice & Prayer* assignments as a family where applicable or desirable.

- If you have young children, read examples and stories from a children's Bible.

If you find other ways of adapting the study to your family, or just want to share what you did and how it worked, I would love to hear from you! Please send me a message through the *Contact Me* page on my website at www.shaunawallace.com.

Individual Study

If you're working through the study alone, use the book for *Individual Study*. Decide how quickly you want to complete it. Is your goal to complete one lesson a day for thirty days in a row? Or will you follow the breakdown of weeks in the study? Whatever it is, write your plan here, and let your written goal be your accountability:

I plan to complete _____ days per week.

I plan to be finished by: _____ (date).

Regardless of the approach you take, group or individual, please note *Appendix B*: *How to Find Something in the Bible* offers suggestions for how to find scriptures by keyword, key phrase or topic. It is by no means exhaustive, but hopefully helpful as you complete some of the exercises in your study.

Week 1

Belonging to Jesus & what He wants of His family.

Days 1-5

Lesson One

Overview of Romans

Romans systematically sets forth the _____ _____ of salvation according to _____ and _____ – "in that order, because right _____ must be established with God before one can live so as to please Him and mediate His blessings to others" (*Expositor's Bible Commentary*).

Chapter 12 begins with _____ so it's important we take a look at what's _____

_____.

Chapter 1-11 = What it _____ to be a Christian.

Eight Great Truths of Salvation

1. There is no unrighteousness with God; He is _____.

2. There is _____ righteous, no, not one; all have _____ and fall short of the glory of God.

3. Salvation is the gift of God through _____ by _____ in Christ to all who _____; it is not by birth, works or the law.

4. In Christ, we are _____ by faith – made _____ _____ _____ _____ never sinned; by faith, the righteousness of Jesus is _____ to all who believe in Him, and we have peace with God.

5. God gives us the _____ _____. We no longer walk according to the _____, but by the Spirit we put to _____ the deeds of the flesh.

6. We won't always choose righteousness; but praise be to God, there is no _____ to those who are in Christ Jesus.

7. As a _____ _____ _____, He foreknew us, predestined us, adopted us, called us, justified us and glorified us; we are His _____.

8. All things _____ _____ for good to those who love God, to those who are _____ _____ according to His purpose.

How to Live as a Christian

Chapter 12 = How to _____ as a Christian.

According to Romans 12:1-8, here's _____ to live for Christ:

1. It requires total _____ (verse 1-2) – "Present your bodies a living sacrifice, holy, pleasing to God, which is your reasonable service"

   a. God saves us once, but we _____ to follow Jesus _____ _____.

   b. Do not be _____ to this world.

   c. Be _____ by the renewing of your mind.

   d. _____ what is the good, acceptable, perfect will of God.

2. It requires a right _____ _____ and _____ – do "not think of (yourself) more highly than (you) ought to think" (verse 3).

3. It requires _____ and functioning as one _____ – "we have many members in one body, but all the members do not have the same function" (verse 4-5).

4. It requires proper _____ of the _____ God gives us (verses 6-8).

The actions we take are made possible _____ of the total dedication, the heart attitude and humility, our unity as one body, and the gifts God's given by _____.

Truths for Moving Forward

1. It's not a matter of a _____ or sticking to certain actions or _____; it's a matter of the _____. It's not about the doing of the _____ thing; it's about the right thing flowing out of a heart full of the _____ of Christ and therefore in love with Him and His ways.

2. When we turn to _____ to gain what only Jesus can give, we rely on our own power and control and have a law or works _____; righteousness by faith requires _____ all power and control to God and then obeying and serving Him.

Days One Through Five

Our passage begins with _____. All other precepts set forth in our passage are _____ of this foundation.

It's not just love, it's _____ love – without _____.

Love is not _____ because it is how people will know we are _____!

17

Day 1

Let love be without hypocrisy.

Scripture

Memorize today's scripture:

Let love be without hypocrisy (Romans 12:9).

It might be helpful to write each day's scripture on an index card. You can use it as a tool to memorize each one, and then you will have an easy way to review as you learn new ones!

Teaching

What a power-packed five words! While it is written as a single exhortation to followers of Jesus, this life app contains two foundational truths on which the entire Christian life is built: "Let love be…" and "…without hypocrisy."

Let's look at this kind of love. It does not refer to romantic or material affections, but to a friendly warmth, kindness and compassion extended to others simply because they are our fellow mankind. It is a welcoming and generous heart that extends good will and charity, serving others with no expectation of profit or return.

It is the love of the second greatest commandment, to love your neighbor as yourself (Mark 12:31).

It is genuine and sincere, unconditional and sacrificial.

It is the love of choice, not feeling, so that even if we don't feel love, we can still extend it.

Without hypocrisy.

Why not just let love be? Isn't that enough? Why the specific instruction that it must be absent hypocrisy?

The two are opposites. Love of the Romans 12:9 kind cannot exist in the face of hypocrisy; one destroys the other.

Jesus specifically addresses hypocrites sixteen times in the gospels, eight times starting with the phrase, "Woe to you!" It is an expression of disapproval, sadness and regret as He exposes the scribes and Pharisees for pretending to be something they aren't, giving the appearance of being or feeling something that isn't really true, concocting a false image or appearance for their own benefit and glory.

The prophet Isaiah describes hypocrites as people who honor God with their lips, but their hearts are far from Him (Mark 7:6). How incredibly accurate!

In Matthew 23:13, Jesus warns of the eternal consequence of hypocrisy: "But woe to you, scribes and Pharisees, hypocrites! For you shut up the kingdom of heaven against men; for you neither go in yourselves, nor do you allow those who are entering to go in."

In the Greek, He's charging them with totally missing the boat in their own ability to enter into the reign of the Messiah, and at the same time, they're obstructing others' ability to see Jesus.

How many times have you heard someone say they won't go to church because Christians are hypocrites?

Hypocrisy hurts; its chief end is to serve oneself by fooling others.

If loving others is the greatest commandment, and others know we are Jesus' disciples by the love we have for one another (John 13:35), then it becomes critical that our love be without pretense. Everything in the light. No faking. Absent ulterior motives and hidden intentions. Being honest, sincere and forthright. Simple and direct. No disguises.

For some of us, this comes naturally. But what about those of us who aren't naturally bent toward mercy, compassion and love for all mankind? Doesn't that make us hypocrites if we act like we love but really don't? Aren't we better off being genuine about our feelings, even if it hurts others? At least we're not being hypocrites!

Not in this case. The love Paul is talking about is not a feeling, but a choice. We don't have to feel love in order to choose it. In fact, it is our love for God and not others that causes us to love them by choice. This undivided love seeks the best for others without consideration of self, that the world would know that the Father sent Jesus, and that He loves us even as He loved His Son.

Jesus sees right through our pretenses, and so do those who watch what we do rather than what we say. Sincere love has the potential to cause others to embrace rather than reject Jesus. Its absence becomes one of the greatest obstacles to the very people who need it most.

Example

Jesus is our greatest example of Romans 12:9 love. Acting in our best interest with no thought of Himself, He left the splendor of heaven, became fully human and then suffered and died to pay the price for the sin of all mankind. Philippians 2:5-8 challenges us to take on His same mindset as we love others:

> Let this mind be in you which was also in Christ Jesus, who, being in the form of God, did not consider it robbery to be equal with God, but made Himself of no reputation, taking the form of a bondservant, and coming in the likeness of men. And being found in appearance as a man, He humbled Himself and became obedient to the point of death, even the death of the cross.

As He walked the earth, teaching and healing, He showed love by speaking truth in love, without judgment or condemnation. One of my favorite encounters is when the scribes and Pharisees bring Jesus a woman caught in adultery in order to trick Him into saying something they can use against Him. (In fact, we'll meet up with this story again on Days 22 and 26.)

Instead of berating her for her obvious sin, He confronts her accusers, challenging the one who knows no sin to throw the first stone at her. When no one does, He says to her, "Neither do I condemn you; go and sin no more" (John 8:11). He doesn't lecture her or tell her how wrong she is. He doesn't shun her or treat her as less than. He simply loves her by speaking truth and telling her how to go forward in His will.

We are to do the same. Our condemnation is not going to win the hearts of those who are living in whatever sin. Because of our own sin, we have no right to throw a stone, no matter how grave another's sins may be: homosexuality, adultery, pornography, murder, abortion, extortion, genocide, slavery. Jesus never said condemn one another as I have condemned you. No, love Him, number one, and then love another as He has loved us. Those are THE GREATEST commandments.

In fact, right after He establishes loving God and loving others as the way to inherit eternal life (Luke 10:25-28), Jesus tells the story of the Good Samaritan, a most powerful illustration of Romans 12:9 love. A Jew traveling the Jericho road falls victim to violent robbers and lies injured and half dead on the side of the road. Those who would be most expected to help him simply pass him by, but a Samaritan, who otherwise would having nothing to do with a Jew at that time, sets aside all differences in order to extend friendly, kind compassion to another human being. He inconveniences himself – time, hardship and finances – to help a man in need.

Let this kind of love be.

Practice & Prayer

1. How do we get this kind of love? It starts with loving Jesus. Read 1 John 4:19. What gives us a love for Jesus?

2. According to 2 Corinthians 5:14-15:

    a. What compels us?

    b. Who do we no longer live for?

    c. Who do we live for?

    d. How does this scripture relate to hypocrisy?

3. What is the greatest challenge you face in loving others?

4. Who is the hardest person for you to love? Why?

Challenge for Today

One of the most famous scriptures on love is 1 Corinthians 13:4-8a. Place your name in each of the blanks below, and then read it aloud.

_____ suffers long and is kind;

_____ does not envy;

_____ does not parade her/himself;

_____ is not puffed up;

_____ does not behave rudely,

_____ does not seek her/his own,

_____ is not provoked,

_____ thinks no evil;

_____ does not rejoice in iniquity

_____ rejoices in the truth;

_____ bears all things,

_____ believes all things,

_____ hopes all things,

_____ endures all things.

_____ 's love never fails.

As you go about your day, when you are frustrated, annoyed, tired, inconvenienced or tempted to act in selfishness, look at this list and *CHOOSE* to respond as the list says you are, even if your feelings tell you different.

Let's Pray: Lord, thank You that You loved us first and sent Your Son, Jesus, to show us what love looks like and to die on the cross for our sins. Compel us by the love of Christ to love others without hypocrisy. Even when we don't feel like it, help us by Your Holy Spirit to choose to extend friendly warmth, kindness and compassion to others simply because they are our fellow mankind. Create in us pure hearts – welcoming and generous – that extend goodwill and charity, serving others with no expectation of profit or return. We commit to love by choice and will not rely on our feelings to rule our actions toward others. In the sweet, holy and mighty name of Jesus, Amen.

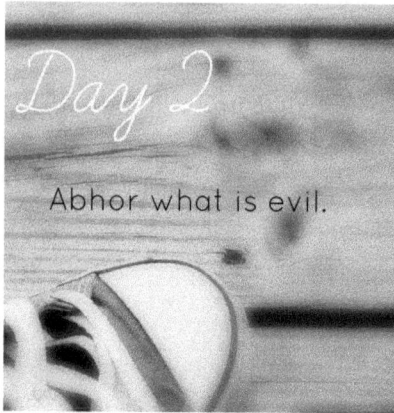

Day 2

Abhor what is evil.

Scripture

Memorize today's scripture:

Abhor what is evil. (Romans 12:9).

Remember, write it on an index card, and don't forget to review what you've already learned!

Teaching

Imagine something you dislike intensely. I mean, this thing absolutely makes you cringe. Picture it in your mind. Perhaps it's a person, behavior or food. Maybe it's exercise, flying or creepy crawly creatures like snakes and cockroaches. Take a moment and write down what it is and your emotional response when you encounter it:

I extremely dislike: _____

When I encounter it, I: _____

_____

_____

Most of us probably do whatever we can to avoid this thing. We might break out in cold sweats and have nightmares about it. Regardless of the source, our emotional response is intense, and our instinct is most likely to get as far away as possible, avoiding it at all cost and retreating when it gets near.

That's what it means to *abhor*. Today's life app is more than just detesting something or even hating it. It's having such horror for something that we completely separate ourselves from it, destroying any union with it and fleeing the other direction!

That's what God wants us to do when we encounter evil.

Most of us equate evil with wickedness or some form of innate immorality that is evidenced by the foul, horrible and revolting actions of the host. Just glance at movie posters or DVD cases for a majority of new releases, and you'll get a pretty good snapshot of evil.

But *evil* also encompasses something that is full of labor, annoyances, hardships, toil and peril. We are to run from this evil too!

I love the way scripture answers scripture, and Ephesians 5:1-18 provides significant clarification as to how we are to abhor evil. In the interest of space, I have not included the entire passage here, so grab your Bible and turn there now. Read the passage once through, and then continue along with me here.

Paul starts the passage telling us to "walk in love" as Christ loved us, and then he names nearly a dozen "unfruitful works of darkness" (we'll look at them in detail in a moment) and urges us not to associate with these behaviors. Don't join those who partake in them, and don't share in what they're doing; in fact, don't even let these things be named among you (verses 3, 7 and 11)! Darkness is their domain, and the ungodly and immoral works of darkness result in nothing but barrenness. Their practices are sterile and unproductive toward any end but desolation.

Why such strong language?

Because before Jesus saved us by grace through faith, we were once darkness, but now we are light in the Lord, and we are to walk as children of light (verse 8). The evidence of the Holy Spirit living in us should be seen in goodness, righteousness and truth (verse 9). Beyond separating ourselves from evil, we are to find out what is acceptable to the Lord (verse 10), carefully striving to diligently do all God instructs and asks us to do (verse 15), not as a means to earn salvation, but as we saw yesterday, because the love of Jesus compels us to do so. We are "to make wise and sacred use of every opportunity for doing good"[1] (verse 16), understand what the will of the Lord is (verse 17) and be filled with the Spirit (verse 18).

What is the will of the Lord? As we learned in our introduction, we are "created in Christ Jesus for good works, which God prepared beforehand that we should walk in them" (Ephesians 2:10).

If we are hanging around with or engaged in any form of evil, we will be bogged down by the labor, annoyances, hardships, toil and peril those things produce in our lives, and we will be unable to do what Jesus created us to do: good works.

The light of Christ will be snuffed out by darkness.

Example

In the Old Testament, the temple was the dwelling place for God's presence. It was holy ground, not to be defiled by any form of evil. It is a type and shadow of our bodies, which are now the temple of the Holy Spirit (1 Corinthians 6:19); our bodies house God's presence (which we'll learn more about on Day 11). When we abhor what is evil, we are treating God's temple as holy, which Jesus took very seriously.

In John chapter two, it is the Passover of the Jews. Jesus is in Jerusalem and finds "in the temple those who sold oxen and sheep and doves, and the money changers doing business" (verse 14). He is furious! He drives them all out with a whip, pours out the money changers' loot and overturns the merchants' tables, demanding, "Take these things away! Do not make My Father's house a house of merchandise!"

He has no tolerance for the evil that is defiling His Father's temple. He abhors it; He drives it out. This is the intensity with which we must hate the evil that defiles us, driving it out with His same passion.

Practice & Prayer

---

[1] Blue Letter Bible. "Dictionary and Word Search for *exagorazō (Strong's 1805)*". Blue Letter Bible. 1996-2013. 14 Jul 2013. http://www.blueletterbible.org/lang/lexicon/lexicon.cfm?Strongs=G1805&t=NKJV.

Using different word choices, Paul starts Ephesians 5:1-18 the same way he starts off Romans 12:9, instructing us to walk in love like Christ. Likewise, he addresses evil next, offering a detailed explanation of different forms of evil. I found eleven. See how many you can find.

1. _____

2. _____

3. _____

4. _____

5. _____

6. _____

7. _____

8. _____

9. _____

10. _____

11. _____

Digging a little deeper into each of these forms of evil, here are all the behaviors this list describes: illicit sex of any kind, including adultery, homosexuality, idolatry and prostitution (as the buyer or seller); lust, which would encompass pornography and anything that would stir a sexual desire for anyone other than a spouse of the opposite sex; extravagant, reckless, wasteful living; impure motives; greedy desires for more; materialism; obscenities; filthy, base or dishonoring language; godless, irreverent, immoral talking; vulgarity; crude or rude joking; vain or idle talk; dishonesty; rebellion against God's will and/or ways; pigheadedness; drunkenness; foolishness; squandering the time God has given.

How does Paul describe these things in verse 11? _____

Where does Paul say these things are done in verse 12? _____

Why do you think these things are done in secret (see verse 12 again)? _____

Why do you think God wants us to stay away from these things? What's their danger? Some are obvious, but others might even seem a little petty.

_____

_____

_____

Many times, what's repulsive to our spirit is cloaked in something attractive to our flesh! What do you think it means on a practical, walk-it-out level that we not even let these things be named among us?

_____

_____

_____

Challenge for Today

Take a few minutes and list any works of darkness in which you partake or that you recognize in those around you. Maybe you listen to music or watch things on television or in movies that glorify unfruitful works of darkness. Perhaps you or the people around you talk about such things, read about them in books, look at images of them online or dabble in discussions about them by text or other forms of social media. You might even be living a double life in secret. Talk about it here.

_____

_____

_____

_____

The goal, of course, would be to separate yourself from all of it, but for today, choose one and have nothing to do with it; don't even allow it to be named among you. At the end of the day, come back here and make a note of what happened. How did you feel? Was it easy or hard? Do you feel like the Lord is urging you to give it up for the long term? What are your fears?

_____

_____

_____

_____

The power to overcome darkness comes only through our relationship with Jesus Christ. As an adopted child of God, go forward in the power of the Holy Spirit and break fellowship with sin.

Let's Pray: Lord, thank You for Your free gift of salvation by grace through faith in Your Son, Jesus Christ. Jesus, we ask You to give us light; expose the shameful works of darkness in which we secretly engage. Bring them to light; no blind spots, Lord. We ask You to show us any way that we are lying to ourselves or being deceived. Please set us free today. Deliver us from evil and the evil one that we would walk in the power of Your Holy Spirit to do the good works You already established for us to do. We ask this in the sweet, holy and mighty name of Jesus, Amen.

Day 3

Cling to what is good.

Scripture

Memorize today's scripture:

Cling to what is good (Romans 12.9).

Write out your index card and review, review, review!

Teaching

When my daughters each turned thirteen, we planned a special purity weekend getaway to talk about what it means to remain emotionally and physically pure for the Lord and for marriage. As an object lesson for one of the sessions, they glued together three sets of two different colors of construction paper and waited varying times before pulling the papers apart. The longer the glue set, the greater the damage to the paper when the girls attempted to separate it. The paper would tear, and entire sections of one color paper would be permanently attached to the other. Once the glue fully dried, they could not separate the papers without destroying both.

This is the idea behind clinging to what is good. We are to fasten ourselves so firmly to what is good that we're set together like cement. To split us would be to destroy both us and the good.

What determined the degree to which the papers were damaged? _____

It was time, right? The more time the paper had to adhere, the harder it was to separate.

If we want to be cemented to good to the point that we are one with it, what do we have to do?

_____

Our time needs to be spent with that which is good.

Who does Mark 10:18 tell us is the only One who is good? _____

If God is the only One who is good, then James 4:8 captures the heart of how we cling to what is good: "Draw near to God and He will draw near to you." In other words, join ourselves to God, who *IS* good, and He who *IS* good will be joined to us. We'll be two pieces of construction paper glued together.

Our time should be spent getting to know God, seeking Him, spending time studying the Bible, which is His word, praying, receiving teaching about Him, His will, His ways and how to serve and please Him. Filling our minds with things that glorify Him in order that we might *become* His good.

This includes spending time with other Christ followers. In John 17:20-23, Jesus prays for those who will believe in Him, "that they all may be one, as You, Father, are in Me, and I in You...I in them, and You in Me; that they may be made perfect in one."

Who and what we hang around with matters. As 1 Corinthians 15:33 warns, "Do not be deceived, 'Evil company corrupts good habits.'" We need to choose wisely, spending the bulk of our time with people who are pursuing and obeying Jesus with all they have. And we want to be that person for others.

Example

Let's look at specific *good* to which scripture says to cling. This certainly is not an exhaustive list, but these ten verses give us a good start. Look up each passage and write in what the verse says to pursue.

1. Psalm 34:14: _____ (We'll have an entire life app on this Day 24!)

2. Micah 6:8: _____, _____ , and _____

3. Romans 14:19: things which make for _____; things by which we _____ others

4. 1 Corinthians 14:1: _____ and _____ _____

5. Ephesians 5:17: _____ the _____ of the _____

6. 1 Thessalonians 5:15: what is good for _____ and for _____

7. 1 Timothy 6:11:

   a. _____

   b. _____

   c. _____

   d. _____

   e. _____

   f. _____

8. 1 Timothy 6:12: the good _____ of _____, and lay hold on

   _____ _____

9. 2 Timothy 2:22: _____, _____, _____, and _____

10. Hebrews 12:14: _____ with all people and _____

Practice & Prayer

How should the idea of time and being "glued" to what we spend our time with affect us in who and where we spend our time?

_____

_____

I've heard it said that we our calendars and checkbooks give us an honest look at what we treasure in life, and I believe that's true. Looking at the facts rather than perceiving things through our good intentions often reveals areas of our lives where we are deceived and need the light of Christ to expose what we need to confess and surrender to the Lord. Like our time, and that to which we cling.

Stop for a minute and list the activities that consume most of your time. Be totally honest. Only the truth sets us free, so if we try to fool ourselves on paper, we are going to live deceived lives.

_____   _____

_____   _____

_____   _____

_____   _____

_____   _____

_____   _____

Now list the people with whom you spend a majority of your time:

_____   _____

_____   _____

_____   _____

_____   _____

_____   _____

The characteristics below define the meaning of the word _good_ in Romans 12:9 as things or people that are:

☐ useful	☐ helpful	☐ beneficial
☐ constructive	☐ valuable	☐ productive
☐ pleasant	☐ agreeable	☐ joyful
☐ happy	☐ excellent	☐ distinguished
☐ upright	☐ honorable	

Now Look back at your lists, and circle the things and people that you can honestly say DO NOT meet the above criteria for good. Again, I'm asking you to be painfully honest for your own good. For me, there are a lot of good things on my plate, but there are others from which I still need to flee. When I circle the people and things from which I need to flee, the list is longer than I'd like to admit.

Challenge for Today

Of the circled items or people on your lists, choose the one you consider to be your "worst offender," the one that distracts you most from clinging to what is good. Make a list of other good things or people with which you could spend that time. When you are tempted or would normally engage with that activity or person, grab your list and do something good in its place.

List your "worst offender" here: _____

List alternative good ideas here:

_____

_____

Just a caution about people in our lives who may not be good for us. We don't want to shun them. We want to be careful to continue to love and show kindness and compassion to them, but when it comes to spending a lot of time with someone, to the point that they are influencing our character, we need to choose wisely. If we are still in the season of raising our families, we need to carefully monitor and influence who our children choose, too.

Let's Pray: Lord, thank You for Your promise to draw near to us when we draw near to You. We want to stick to You like glue. Please give us eyes to see and hearts to understand what is good in Your eyes. Holy Spirit, give us wisdom, power and courage to spend our time pursuing good, even when it's hard. We ask these things in the sweet, holy and mighty name of Jesus, Amen.

Day 4

Be kindly affectionate to one another with brotherly love.

Scripture

Memorize today's scripture:

Be kindly affectionate to one another with brotherly love (Romans 12:10).

We're starting a new verse today. Did you master verse nine already? Write today's segment on your index card and review, review, review!

Teaching

Sibling rivalry. It's as old as Cain and Abel, the first brothers ever to walk the earth. It seems as if the moment that new little brother or sister enters this world, it's on! Jockeying for priority, love, attention or more or less of something becomes a driving M.O. The one who feels the scales are tipped in another's favor is going to be the one to make sure things equal out! All bets are off!

In many families, hurtful words, angry faces, slammed doors, physical retaliation and tearful tattling become a normal and exhausting aspect of a parent's daily routine. Even though most siblings really do love each other and have as many or more loving moments, an observer who witnesses family squabbles might never know it by the way they treat each other, and they might walk away with a negative impression of the parents and the family as a whole.

Sadly, the same can be said of the church.

When we are saved by grace through faith in Jesus, we become the children of God (Romans 8:16). We are of the bloodline of Christ, joint heirs, brothers and sisters in Christ.

When Paul tells us in verse ten to "be kindly affectionate to one another with brotherly love," he's comparing the way we are to cherish our spiritual siblings to the natural tenderness and reciprocal love most typically shown between husbands and wives and parents and children.

What if your family didn't or doesn't look like this even on a good day? Some of us have no reference for this kind of family love. Let me assure you, as your perfect heavenly Father, the Lord will show you and what this kind of love looks like and how to have it! Look to Him as your Father, and trust Him to teach you.

Because of who God is as our Father, this life app instructs us to extend this gentle, family-type love to other followers of Jesus, even when, as in a typical family, we don't always agree on everything, things aren't going our way or we're just not getting along. We're not going to like all our brothers and sisters in Christ, but we are called to love them all!

If the litmus test of a disciple of Jesus is the love we have for one another, how we treat each other is of great importance because of the resulting conclusions others draw about our heavenly Father and the church family as a whole. It goes back to Day 1 when we talked about the importance of loving without hypocrisy and the negative effect our inconsistencies have on people peeking in from the outside.

As His followers, we are a picture of Christ. What people see speaks louder than anything we say, so what are our relationships with our brethren preaching of Jesus? Does our behavior entice or offend?

Even when we disagree, we must guard against letting it divide us.

Where I live, there are probably a hundred churches within a ten-mile radius. No exaggeration. I don't think it's because buildings are bursting at the seams from the multitudes who see what we have, consequently place their faith in Jesus Christ and then flood the doors of their local church. It seems more likely because of division in the family of Christ. Someone disagrees with something and decides to start a new church, and existing church goers move from one building to the next.

What does this say about the body of Christ? When those who don't yet know Jesus notice the bickering and discord among His followers, what conclusions will they draw?

As we saw yesterday, Jesus prayed to the Father for unity because He knew the danger of division (John 17:20-23). Our lack of unity is the enemy of the gospel. If we are at odds, our testimony as the church is tainted. Are we not seeing the reality of that today?

Paul beseeches the Ephesian church "to walk worthy of the calling with which you were called, with all lowliness and gentleness, with longsuffering, bearing with one another in love, endeavoring to keep the unity of the Spirit in the bond of peace" (Ephesians 4:1-3). These words apply as much to us today as they did to the Ephesians back then, and here's why: "There is one body and one Spirit, just as you were called in one hope of your calling; one Lord, one faith, one baptism; one God and Father of all, who is above all, and through all, and in you all" (verses 4-6).

We have a calling. It is a worthy calling, and we must conduct ourselves in a manner as worthy as the calling itself: unified as one body, with one Spirit, one hope, one Lord, one faith, one baptism and one God and Father, even when we don't share the same opinion or interpretation of certain scriptures.

Because we are recipients of our heavenly Father's great mercy, we are to extend that mercy to our brethren, without judgment, "for judgment is without mercy to the one who has shown no mercy. Mercy triumphs over judgment" (James 2:13). To show mercy is always better than judgment.

We have the same Daddy. We are family. Just as we might bicker but hopefully don't divide our families, we need to be indivisible as a Christian family and take care of our own, tenderly, lovingly and mutually.

People are watching our every move looking for sincerity. How we treat each other is the pulpit from which a sincere gospel is preached.

Example

Look up the following scriptures for examples of what it means to be kindly affectionate to one another with brotherly love, and then rate how you feel you or your family are doing in that area: 1 is lousy, and 10 is pretty darn good. Be honest! It's okay if you're a 1, and it's okay if you're a 10. Notice, there are no 5s or 6s. Those are copout choices. No neutral here! You're either on one side of the scale or the other.

Before we begin, let me stress that this exercise is not meant to bring condemnation, for there is no condemnation for those who are in Christ (Romans 8:1)! Rather, it's to be a reality check so we can seek to improve at being kindly affectionate to one another with brotherly love and line our priorities up with Jesus'. If the Holy Spirit convicts us, then that's a good thing! Take the conviction from the Lord as direction to move forward, but leave the condemnation the devil wants to use to weigh you down!

Matthew 25:35-36:

Feeding the hungry.

1 2 3 4 * 7 8 9 10**

Giving drink to the thirsty.

1 2 3 4 * 7 8 9 10**

Taking in strangers.

1 2 3 4 * 7 8 9 10**

Clothing the naked.

1 2 3 4 * 7 8 9 10**

Visiting the sick.

1 2 3 4 * 7 8 9 10**

Visiting those in prison.

1 2 3 4 * 7 8 9 10**

Luke 22:32:

Praying for and strengthening our brethren.

1 2 3 4 * 7 8 9 10**

John 19:25-27:

Taking other believers into our homes as our own, short or long term.

1 2 3 4 * 7 8 9 10**

32

Acts 2:44-45:

Sharing everything we have to meet the needs of our family in Christ.

1   2   3   4   ***   7   8   9   10

Ephesians 4:1-3:

Walking in lowliness, gentleness and longsuffering.

1   2   3   4   ***   7   8   9   10

Bearing with one another in love.

1   2   3   4   ***   7   8   9   10

Keeping the unity of the spirit in the bond of peace.

1   2   3   4   ***   7   8   9   10

Hebrews 10:24-25:

Observing others with an eye to sharpen one another in love for good works.

1   2   3   4   ***   7   8   9   10

Attending and getting plugged in to church, serving and exhorting one another.

1   2   3   4   ***   7   8   9   10

James 1:27:

Visiting orphans.

1   2   3   4   ***   7   8   9   10

Visiting widows.

1   2   3   4   ***   7   8   9   10

2 Peter 1:7:

Showing kindness, even when irritated or offended.

1   2   3   4   ***   7   8   9   10

Practice & Prayer

I would venture to say the root of most of our "lousy" scores is some form of selfishness or self-seeking. It's inconvenient, uncomfortable and requires too much sacrifice to put someone else and their needs before our own. We might console ourselves by insisting someone else already has that covered. Or some of us may hold our possessions tightly, working hard to maintain what we have as we strive for more or better or nicer.

So many times, we are so busy with our lives that we miss needs all around us; therefore, they go unmet by the very people God has called to be a blessing to others: us. We might get too busy for church, going only when it's convenient rather than because it's our lifeline, or perhaps we go but don't get involved because it requires too much or it's too risky. We may even view needs and commitments through the lens of what we might get from it rather than the perspective of what God might have for us to give: the what's-in-it-for-Him factor.

Even as God is doing a deep work in my heart to heighten my awareness and increase my compassion and response to the hurts and needs of others, too much of this is too close for comfort for me. What about you? What stops you from extending kindly affection to one another with brotherly love? Jot your thoughts below.

_____

_____

_____

_____

Challenge for Today

Review your evaluation of yourself, paying particular attention to the scales where you scored more toward lousy. Take a moment and ask the Lord in which of those areas He has a way for you to be kindly affectionate to another with brotherly love today. Listen for His answer as you look back over your scales. As He shows you what to do, do it. Today. What is the Lord showing you?

_____

_____

_____

_____

When your act of kindness is complete, make a note here of what you did and what happened. How did you feel? How did the person respond? What did you learn about yourself? What did you learn about God? How can you continue to extend kindness as a daily habit in other low-scoring areas?

Write your thoughts here.

_____

_____

_____

_____

Let's Pray: Lord, as others peek into the heart of Christ by watching how we as Your children behave toward one another, let them witness kindly affection in everything we do. As our heavenly Father, teach us what Your divine family should look like and how we should treat each other. Give us tender hearts to recognize and respond to the needs of our brothers and sisters in Christ, extending the same consideration and compassion to them as You would have us do to someone in our natural family. In the sweet, holy and mighty name of Jesus, Amen.

Day 5

In honor giving preference to one another.

Scripture

Memorize today's scripture:

In honor giving preference to one another (Romans 12:10).

We're wrapping up our second verse of scripture memory today. How are you doing? Keep adding each day's life app to your index cards and review. You will get this! It will be worth it!

Teaching

Today's life app is the how to do of yesterday's what to do. *Give preference* is the action we are to take, but the preceding prepositional phrase is the game changer. It is the how of the how! Let me explain, because when I went through this study as a participant for the first time, the Lord showed me the importance of our first two words– *in honor* – and He blew me away.

Initially, today's teaching focused only on the idea of *give preference* and what it means to walk that out, but in completing yesterday's *Challenge for Today*, the Lord reminded me of a truth He's made clear to me for a while now: the possession I am most challenged to part with in showing kindness is my time. With that fresh on my mind, I read through today's *Teaching*, and it occurred to me that I hadn't considered the presence or significance of *in honor* as an adverbial clause modifying *give preference*. As my husband would say, "It's epic!"

When I looked up *in honor* in the Greek, I literally had to sit back and take a moment to marvel at the Lord and the intricacies of His word. Oh, if I had the ability to play a drum roll right here! Imagine one for me, along with a suspenseful pause as I prepare to reveal the Greek word for *honor*...

> *timē*

The very thing that can be my greatest challenge – finding and sacrificing my time to extend brotherly love to others – stared back at me as the key to how we do it: with our time! As if that didn't blow my mind to pieces, the definition brings everything into even clearer focus. *Timē* (pronounced tē-mā') can refer to the value of someone or something as determined by the price paid for it, or it can refer to respect manifested or regard due someone because of rank, office or title.[2]

---

[2] "Greek Lexicon :: G5092 (NKJV)." Blue Letter Bible. Web. 28 Feb, 2016.
<http://www.blueletterbible.org/lang/lexicon/lexicon.cfm?Strongs=G5092&t=NKJV>.

In Paul's time, to put a price on someone purchased would likely refer to a slave. When he writes in 1 Corinthians 6:20 that we "were bought at a price," he's referring to the high price Jesus paid for our redemption and salvation from slavery to sin. God put such a high value on us that He sent His Son to die for us. Jesus paid for us with His shed blood! We now have the title "child of God," and so does every one of our brethren. So because of the high price God puts on them, we should value and regard them just as highly; therefore, in *timē* giving preference to them!

So let's look at the Greek meaning behind *preference*: "to go before and show the way, to go before and lead, to go before as a leader."[3]

Paul is telling us to be the one to make the first move! No waiting for someone else to do their part first. No waiting for our needs to be met before we think we can meet someone else's. No holding out for something else to fall into place first so we feel we are finally able to give and serve.

The Lord taught me and James preference in the early years of our marriage. We were insecure, volatile, financially stressed, emotionally bankrupt spiritual newborns, and our marriage was in shambles. We were miserable! All that mattered to us was what the other person was or wasn't doing and what needs of ours were or weren't being met. It was an extremely difficult time, but in the Lord's eternal faithfulness, He extended tremendous grace and mercy to us.

One of the life lessons He secured in us as He taught us preference was the importance of trusting *Him* enough to leave the other person in His hands, freeing us to be consumed with pleasing Him as the wife or husband He wanted us to be. We had to let go of the consequences, what we saw as our rights and whether or not the other person deserved God-honoring treatment or not.

God made it unquestionably clear that what the other person did or didn't do wasn't our concern; it was His. And His business with each of us was our obedience to *Him*, not whether or not we were holding the other person accountable for what we thought was their responsibility.

In order for our marriage to work, we had to set aside our fears of not getting what we thought we wanted, needed or deserved and totally trust in the Lord to be God of our lives and of each others' hearts, attitudes, thoughts and actions. It was HARD, but in reality, it was the easiest answer ever because the burden rolled onto Jesus, where it belongs, and we were free to simply obey God as an act of worship in our relationship with each other. When we did, He worked miracles in our marriage and our family. He supplied all our needs. He healed hurts and restored loving-kindness and tenderness.

We learned the going before of *preference*, and when practiced with sincerity, *preference* often leads to the reciprocal or mutual nature of one another whereby "no one seek(s) his own, but each one the other's well-being" (1 Corinthians 10:24).

Together, "in honor give preference" means this: We respectfully submit to Jesus, who paid a high price for us because of our value to Him; we esteem Him highly, and our respect for Him is manifested to His children. We give of our time, because we put a high value on our brethren, because of the high price He paid for them and the value He places on them. He leads the way in this, and so we follow in His steps, going first because that's what He did.

---

[3] Blue Letter Bible. "Dictionary and Word Search for *proēgeomai (Strong's 4285)*". Blue Letter Bible. 1996-2013. 5 Aug 2013. www.blueletterbible.org/lang/lexicon/lexicon.cfm?Strongs=G4285&t=NKJV.

Example

Jesus lived today's life app, continually modeling selfless living. A great example is in Mark chapter six, when Jesus and His disciples can't even find time to eat for the comings and goings of the multitudes. So He says to them, "Come aside by yourselves to a deserted place and rest a while" (verse 31).

When the multitudes follow, Jesus does not turn them away. Instead, He is "moved with compassion for them, because they were like sheep not having a shepherd. So He began to teach them many things" (verse 34). He sees their need and puts aside His. When His disciples want Jesus to send the people away to find food for themselves, Jesus instead feeds five thousand men with five loaves and two fish. A miracle.

With His time, He gives preference.

Even when no one would have blamed Him for demanding a little "me" time, He continued to pour Himself out in preference to others. He lived Philippians 2:3-4:

> Let nothing be done through selfish ambition or conceit, but in lowliness of mind let each esteem others better than himself. Let each of you look out not only for his own interests, but also for the interests of others.

It is directly after these two verses that Paul tells us to have the mind of Christ, which was our *Example* on Day 1 – the mind of Christ, who humbled Himself in obedience to the point of death on a cross. In the face of what Jesus did for us, how can we not do what He asks of us? How can we accept salvation by grace through faith, the promise of eternal life with Him, as well as all His promises to us for our life here on earth, and then deny Him the denying of ourselves that's required to give preference to others?

Because He first loved us, we are compelled by the love of Christ to follow after Him, doing what He did, in honor giving preference to others.

Practice & Prayer

As we learn to honor others in preference, it will require a bit of sacrifice and suffering. Maybe even a lot. In his letter to early Christians, Peter encourages us to see temporary sufferings in light of eternal glory. Look up 1 Peter 1:3-7 in the NKJV. Read the passage, and then answer the following questions.

1. According to God's abundant mercy through the resurrection of Jesus, to what are we begotten (verse 3)?

   _____

   Based on the Greek meaning of *begotten*, Peter is saying we're born anew to a changed mind by which we now live a life conformed to God's will, and the result is living hope!

2. How does verse 4 describe our living hope? _____

   _____

3. What else are we promised in verse 5? _____

   _____

4. According to verse 6, why is this living hope important?

   _____

5. What reason does verse 7 give for the various trials of verse 6?

   _____

   _____

6. How does Peter describe genuine faith in verse 7?

   _____

   More precious, or *timios* in the Greek, which, you might have already guessed, comes from the root *timē*! Our faith should be esteemed and held more dear than gold, for gold perishes, but our faith, when tested by fire and found genuine, "may be found to praise, _____, and glory at the revelation of Jesus Christ" (fill in the blank according to verse 7).

   Guess what the Greek word is for *honor*? Yes! *Timē*! If we substitute the meaning *value* for *honor*, it would read: "may be found to praise, *value*, and glory at the revelation of Jesus Christ"!

Now look up Revelation 5:12. Who is worthy "to receive power and riches and wisdom, and strength hand honor and glory and blessing"?

_____

According to 1 Peter 2:7, what does Peter call Jesus to us who believe? _____

We will give preference and therefore serve what we value. If Jesus is precious to us, then we will make what is precious to Him a priority in our lives.

First Peter 3:7 addresses husbands and wives, but it contains a truth powerfully applicable to our life app today. What basis does Peter give for husbands giving honor to or valuing their wives (other than as to a weaker vessel)?

_____

Isn't this true of us all? We are all heirs together of the grace of life. Jesus is precious to us! The value of our faith – our trust in the Lord – is more precious than gold, and our faith enables us to value others, in honor giving preference to them, even when it requires momentary sacrifice or suffering.

Challenge for Today

What is a scenario in a typical day when you would normally put yourself first with your time? Maybe it's with a brother or sister, a spouse or parent, grandparent or boss. Perhaps it's with your friends, children or grandchildren. Write it out here.

_____

_____

_____

_____

When faced with that circumstance today, instead of protecting your interests and making sure it goes your way first, give preference to the other person. If the opportunity doesn't present itself, create one in which you take the time and initiative to put someone else first. Be sure to come back and write down what you did and what happened. How did you feel when you put someone else first? Did you get the response you wanted? Did their response affect your opinion or satisfaction from honoring them?

_____

_____

_____

_____

Let's Pray: Lord, help us to recognize our selfishness and fear and fully trust in You. We know You alone are trustworthy. We know in You alone are hope, strength, deliverance and protection. We declare in the name of Jesus by the power of the Holy Spirit that we trust You, and in honor, we will strive to give preference to one another that You may be glorified. In the sweet, holy and mighty name of Jesus, Amen.

Reflect & Review

Take a few minutes to look back through this week's challenges. Did you remember to write down what happened when you completed your challenges? Are there any you never got to or want to redo? Is there anything you want to make note of as a record of what you see the Lord doing or something you otherwise don't want to forget? Use this space for your thoughts.

_____

_____

_____

_____

_____

_____

_____

_____

I'd like to finish and/or repeat:

_____

_____

_____

_____

_____

_____

Week 2

The inside job: heart attitudes and the who of our hope.

Days 6-11

Lesson Two

The Inside Job

Walking the talk is an _____ job determined by our heart attitudes and where we place our _____. This week, we will learn that we are to walk the talk "not lagging in diligence, fervent in spirit, serving the Lord; rejoicing in hope, patient in tribulation, continuing steadfastly in prayer" (Romans 12:11-12).

Two Essential Truths

Our six life apps can be divided into two groups of three; the essence can be stated in two truths:

1. TRUTH ONE: In Christ, we are no longer slaves to sin, but we are Christ's _____, free to passionately pursue good works with _____; and

2. TRUTH TWO: Our _____ in Christ is the source of the patience we'll need in the face of persecution; continual _____ is our source of help and steadfastness.

The relationship among our life apps is not so much progressive as it is _____. We don't move from one to the other in successive order, but rather they all _____-_____ in a web with one common thread: _____.

The center of the web is Jesus, and the key to unwavering hope is the _____ or _____ of our desire. If our hope is in Jesus and Him _____, then our heart attitudes will reflect our hope in Him.

Choosing Diligence

While we are saved by grace, diligence is a _____, and feelings will sometimes _____ the choice to be diligent.

Sometimes, the choice to hope in Christ and passionately and diligently serve Him in patience and prayer may precede _____ of passion, diligence, patience and faith.

The key to diligence is _____ _____ in our walk with God, even on the days we don't feel like it (see Philippians 3:12-14).

Pressing on also plays a role in being fervent in spirit, which is to be _____ for good works. Not good works _____ salvation, but good works _____ of salvation.

> "For we are His workmanship, created in Christ Jesus for good works, which God prepared beforehand that we should walk in them" (Ephesians 2:10).

When Our Walk Requires Waiting

When our walk requires patience, and we find ourselves waiting on God, the_____ to wait and ability to persevere with diligence depends on the _____ of our hope – the thing we're waiting on to be _____, especially in times of tribulation or _____.

Our hope will always be _____ when it is in Jesus; if the object of our hope is in anything else, we will end up _____.

As long as we maintain a _____ of hope in anyone or anything but Jesus, we will not _____ place our hope in Him.

Hope-filled Heart Attitudes

Of our hope in Christ, scripture says:

Christ is us is our hope of _____ (Colossians 1:27).

Hope in Christ is an _____ of the soul, sure and steadfast (Hebrews 6:19).

We can have unwavering hope in Christ because God is _____ (Hebrews 10:23).

The hope we have is a _____ hope "through the resurrection of Jesus Christ from the dead" (1 Peter 1:3).

Jesus is living hope; He produces _____ - _____ heart attitudes. When we choose to put our hope in Christ and Christ alone, He enables us to wait patiently on God with a _____ heart. A perfect heart is not defined as without _____, but perfect as in being _____ God's; It is a heart whose _____ is in Christ alone.

Day 6

Not lagging in diligence.

Scripture

Memorize today's scripture:

Not lagging in diligence (Romans 12:11).

Let's start another verse today. Review verses nine and ten, and then add this segment to your index cards. It's just four words. You can do it!

Teaching

If *lagging* was a car, it would be running idle without any power applied to the pedal, gears disengaged, aimlessly passing time.

If *lagging* was a disease, it would be slow to develop and slow to be healed. It would be painless and hard to discover, much like cancer that often grows undetected until it's too late. The disease of *lagging* sneaks up on you.

If *lagging* was a person, he would be apathetic and indifferent, lacking energy and interest in all matters, not bothering with anything at all, frivolously wasting time and unlikely to engage in anything productive.

In the Greek, *lagging* actually means slothful, conjuring up images of a slow-moving mammal that sleeps or rests fifteen to eighteen hours a day, dragging itself where it needs to go. The sloth's inertness makes it a healthy habitat for pests, like moths, beetles, cockroaches, fungi and algae. Its best defense is camouflage because running away just isn't an option. Sloths blend in and rarely move, sometimes living in the same tree for up to thirty years. In many of the places where they live, they are the majority, making up for as much as two-thirds of the mammal population.

This paints a picture of what our lives will look like, too, when we lag.

The root of *lagging* is to feel loath, be averse, unwilling, reluctant or wary and opposed to anything that requires effort. It may manifest as hesitating and procrastinating until you just can't get away with it any longer.

Thus, Paul warns us against being slothful with a dislike for work or any form of physical or spiritual exertion, wasting time and ineffective at carrying things out or putting them into effect. It requires nothing of us to be slothful, but the consequences cost much: "He who is slothful in his work is a brother to him who is a great destroyer" (Proverbs 18:9).

Diligence, on the other hand, requires much.

If it was a car, it would be a racecar, revving and maneuvering with determination to do whatever it takes to be the first across finish line.

If *diligence* was a person, he would be an entrepreneur, making haste to intently accomplish, promote or strive after his goals and objectives. He would interest himself most earnestly in whatever was required for his success, running his business with care and attention to how it's supposed to be done.

If *diligence* was a creature, it would be an ant, persistent and hard-working day and night, day after day, never stopping, always laboring for its survival and for the benefit of its colony.

Diligence is being quick to obey, like Isaiah, who responded to the Lord in a vision, "Here am I! Send me" (Isaiah 6:8). Or Abraham, who "rose early in the morning" to obey God's command to sacrifice the son God had promised him (Genesis 22:3). Like Samuel, who answered God, "Speak, for Your servant hears" (1 Samuel 3:10).

The things the Lord asks of us can be difficult; the things that please Him go against our selfish nature and require us to do hard things, not just once, but persistently. If we are not lagging in diligence, then we are vigorous and active. Alert.

Talk is cheap. Our actions – or our walk, as is our focus these thirty days – are truly telling. Consider these scriptures:

> In all labor there is profit, but idle chatter leads only to poverty (Proverbs 14:23).

> For every idle word men may speak, they will give account of it in the day of judgment (Matthew 12:36).

> Therefore, to him who knows to do good and does not do it, to him it is sin (James 4:17).

It's time we kick it into high gear with the power of the Holy Spirit and do God's good with diligence (Galatians 6:9), busying ourselves with "things that accompany salvation" (Hebrews 6:9), "that each one of you show the same diligence to the full assurance of hope until the end, that you do not become sluggish, but imitate those who through faith and patience inherit the promises" (Hebrews 6:11-12).

The cost of diligence is well worth it:

> But also for this very reason, **giving all diligence**, add to your faith virtue, to virtue knowledge, to knowledge self-control, to self-control perseverance, to perseverance godliness, to godliness brotherly kindness, and to brotherly kindness love. For if these things are yours and abound, you will be neither barren nor unfruitful in the knowledge of our Lord Jesus Christ. For he who lacks these things is shortsighted, even to blindness, and has forgotten that he was cleansed from his old sins. Therefore, brethren, **be even more diligent** to make your call and election sure, <u>**for if you do these things you will never stumble; for so an entrance will be supplied to you abundantly into the everlasting kingdom of our Lord and Savior Jesus Christ**</u> (2 Peter 1:5-11, all emphasis added).

Example

If lagging is dragging, then we need to do the opposite. In 2 Corinthians 8:1-4, Paul speaks of the joyful, liberal giving of the Macedonian churches, even in the face of trials and persecution. In verses 5-17, he presents eight principles we can apply to excel in diligence and "abound in grace."

8 Principles to Excel in Diligence and Abound in Grace

1. First give yourself to the Lord, and then give to others by His will.

   > And not only as we had hoped, but they first gave themselves to the Lord, and then to us by the will of God (verse 5).

2. Do everything abounding in faith, speech, knowledge, diligence, love and grace.

   > But as you abound in everything – in faith, in speech, in knowledge, in all diligence, and in your love for us – see that you abound in this grace also (verse 7).

3. Operate from sincerity of heart, the evidence of which is the diligence of others.

   > I speak not by commandment, but I am testing the sincerity of your love by the diligence of others (verse 8).

4. Follow the example of Jesus, who gave up the glory of heaven to become "poor" so we might become spiritually rich.

   > For you know the grace of our Lord Jesus Christ, that though He was rich, yet for your sakes He became poor, that you through His poverty might become rich (verse 9).

5. Follow things through to the end.

   > And in this I give advice: It is to your advantage not only to be doing what you began and were desiring to do a year ago; but now you also must complete the doing of it; that as there was a readiness to desire it, so there also may be a completion out of what you have (verse 10-11).

6. Respond to God with willingness and without excuse.

   > For if there is first a willing mind, it is accepted according to what one has, and not according to what he does not have (verse 12).

7. Give generously to supply others' needs.

   > For I do not mean that others should be eased and you burdened; but by an equality, that now at this time your abundance may supply their lack, that their abundance also may supply your lack – that there may be equality (verse 13-14).

8. As God puts diligence in you, go beyond the bare minimum.

   > But thanks be to God who puts the same earnest care for you into the heart of Titus. For he not only accepted the exhortation, but being more diligent, he went to you of his own accord (verse 16-17).

Practice & Prayer

Second Timothy 2:15 instructs us to "be diligent to present yourself approved to God, a worker who does not need to be ashamed, rightly dividing the word of truth." As we've seen, scripture has a lot to say about our laziness or diligence. Both have consequences, and because of our free will, we choose which we will embrace as our lifestyle. Which will be our exception and which will be our rule? We are all going to have lazy days, but are we going to choose a lazy lifestyle, one marked by a lack of diligence?

Look up each scripture below and write the consequence for laziness and the consequence for diligence under each heading. Not all scriptures have content for both columns, so just fill in whatever you find.

SCRIPTURE	Laziness	Diligence
Proverbs 10:4		
Proverbs 12:24		
Proverbs 12:27		
Proverbs 13:4		
Proverbs 15:19		
Proverbs 19:15		
Proverbs 20:13		
Proverbs 21:5		
Proverbs 21:25		
Proverbs 26:16		
Ecclesiastes 10:18		

Challenge for Today

In which areas of your life are you practicing diligence or does diligence come easy? Name them here.

_____

_____

_____

_____

In which areas of your life are you struggling with diligence? Name them here.

_____

_____

_____

Choose one of the areas in which you are struggling. What can you do TODAY to take a step toward diligence in that specific area? Name it here and then do it.

_____

_____

_____

No matter your struggles, always keep in mind the Lord's assurance in 2 Corinthians 12:9, ""My grace is sufficient for you, for My strength is made perfect in weakness."

Let's Pray: Lord, thank You that You make diligence possible, and when we fall short, Your grace is sufficient. We need You, Lord. Help us today to remain faithful to You, diligent in doing what You ask us to do. In the sweet, holy and mighty name of Jesus, Amen.

Day 7

Fervent in spirit.

Scripture

Memorize today's scripture:

Fervent in spirit (Romans 12:11).

Today's life app is just three words. Take a minute to master them now, and then see if you can recite our passage from the beginning. Add today's section to your index cards so it's easy to keep reviewing.

Teaching

One of the reasons I limit my news intake is for my own emotional well-being. My children appreciate it too, mostly because they don't know what to do with me when I begin ranting at the television in an attempt to knock some sense into the people making the news. It simply brings my blood to a boil!

That is the epitome of *fervent*. It is having such an intense passion for what is good or bad that your fervor overflows like boiling water.

To be *fervent in spirit* with a lower-case *s* is for our thoughts, knowledge, desires, feelings, decisions and actions to be an outflow of our intense passion for what is good and bad. It is for zeal to animate and govern who we are and what we do.

The object of our passion becomes the source of our zealousness, and Titus 2:14 tells us Jesus "gave Himself for us, that He might redeem us from every lawless deed and purify for Himself His own special people, zealous for good works."

Not only has Jesus paid the price and set us free from sin, defilement, wickedness and guilt, but He is adapting us in nature and character to be known as His by our intense passion for good works – the genuine, sacrificial, praiseworthy undertakings that occupy our time and energy as a result of the work Jesus has done and is doing in us.

Why good works? Here are six scriptural reasons to consider:

1. They are the reason we were created in Christ Jesus (as we learned on Day 2).

    "For we are His workmanship, created in Christ Jesus for good works, which God prepared beforehand that we should walk in them" (Ephesians 2:10).

2. They are the fruit by which we're known as belonging to Jesus and a measure of our fruitfulness.

   "A tree is known by its fruit" (Matthew 12:33). Therefore, "let our people also learn to maintain good works, to meet urgent needs, that they may not be unfruitful" (Titus 3:14).

3. They affect our reputation and respect.

   "The good works of some are clearly evident, and those that are otherwise cannot be hidden" (1 Timothy 5:25). Therefore, "in all things (show) yourself to be a pattern of good works; in doctrine showing integrity, reverence, incorruptibility, sound speech that cannot be condemned, that one who is an opponent may be ashamed, having nothing evil to say of you" (Titus 2:7-8).

4. They determine our standing and influence with authority and render the ignorant speechless.

   "Therefore submit yourselves to every ordinance of man for the Lord's sake, whether to the king as supreme, or to governors, as to those who are sent by him for the punishment of evildoers and for the praise of those who do good. For this is the will of God, that by doing good you may put to silence the ignorance of foolish men" (1 Peter 2:13-15). Therefore, "Be subject to rulers and authorities, to obey, to be ready for every good work" (Titus 3:1). "Do what is good, and you will have praise from the same" (Romans 13:3).

5. They are good and profitable.

   "This is a faithful saying, and these things I want you to affirm constantly, that those who have believed in God should be careful to maintain good works. These things are good and profitable to men" (Titus 3:8). Therefore, "let them do good, that they may be rich in good works, ready to give, willing to share, storing up for themselves a good foundation for the time to come, that they may lay hold on eternal life" (1 Timothy 6:18-19).

6. They are pleasing to the Lord and bring Him glory.

   "Let your light so shine before men, that they may see your good works and glorify your Father in heaven" (Matthew 5:16).

The key to becoming fervent in spirit is 2 Timothy 3:16-17: "All Scripture is given by inspiration of God, and is profitable for doctrine, for reproof, for correction, for instruction in righteousness, that the man of God may be complete, thoroughly equipped for every good work."

We must fall in love with the word of God, allowing its truths to light a fire within us and equip us for what He has for us to do.

Even as we stumble and fall short of what God expects, as I do more often than I'd like to admit, we can be sure of one thing, and that is His faithfulness. He has begun His good work in us, and Philippians 1:6 assures us He will complete it until the day of Jesus Christ, for it is God who is "able to make all grace abound toward you, that you, always having all sufficiency in all things, may have an abundance for every good work" (2 Corinthians 9:8).

Example

The phrase *fervent in spirit* is used only one other time in the New Testament to describe an eloquent Alexandrian Jew named Apollos. Grab your Bible and read Acts 18:25-28, 1 Corinthians 3:5-6, 4:6 and 16:12, filling in the blanks below to build a profile of someone who is fervent in spirit. (Remember, you might find it helpful to look these verses up in the NKJV.)

1. He had been _____ in the _____ ____ _____ _____ (Acts 18:25).

2. He _____ and _____ accurately the things of the Lord (Acts 18:25).

3. He spoke _____ in the synagogue (Acts 18:26).

4. He greatly _____ those who had _____ _____ _____

    (Acts 18:27).

5. He vigorously _____ the Jews publicly (Acts 18:28).

6. He showed from the _____ that Jesus is the _____ (Acts 18:28).

7. He was a _____, which in the Greek means he executed the commands of Christ as a

    servant of the King (1 Corinthians 3:5).

8. He _____ the _____ Paul planted (1 Corinthians 3:6).

9. He set the example of not thinking beyond _____ _____ _____, that

    none will be _____ _____ or think highly of oneself above _____

    (1 Corinthians 4:6).

10. He was _____ to come, but would come when he had a _____

    time (1 Corinthians 16:12).

What do these scriptures about Apollos teach you about being fervent in spirit? Which do you see in yourself and which do you see lacking?

_____

_____

_____

_____

_____

Practice & Prayer

What are you intensely passionate about? If you're not sure, study the evidence of how you spend your money and/or free time or what most occupies your thoughts.

_____

_____

_____

Would you say the object of your zeal produces good works? Explain your answer.

_____

_____

_____

Based on today's lesson, circle the areas that are your strengths, and place a star next to the ones that are a struggle.

consistency	instruction in God's word	integrity
courageous obedience	respect for authority	incorruptible convictions
profitable works	bold, scripturally sound speech	respected reputation
	humility	

Challenge for Today

Of the items you starred, choose the one you believe presents your greatest opportunity for growth in good works.

Name it here: _____

According to 2 Timothy 3:16-17 and Acts 18:25, God's word is critical to being fervent in spirit and equipped for good works. Using the concordance in the back of your Bible or an online resource, look up three scriptures that instruct you in the area you named as your greatest opportunity for growth. (Refer to *Appendix B: How to Find Something in the Bible* for suggestions, if needed.)

Copy the scriptures below. Be sure to include the book, chapter and verse for where you find them.

1. _____

_____

_____

2. _____

_____

_____

3. _____

_____

_____

Take one of those scripture and turn it into an action step you can take today. Name it here and then do it. Today.

_____

_____

Once you've completed your challenge, come back and write down what happened. Did you do it? Was it easy or hard? How did it feel? What did you learn? What is God showing you?

_____

_____

_____

_____

Let's Pray: Lord, make us complete in every good work to do Your will, working in us what is well-pleasing in Your sight, through Jesus Christ, to whom be glory forever and ever (Hebrews 13:21). We trust in You, Lord. Help us to lean not on our own understanding, but to acknowledge You in all our ways. Direct our paths toward the good works You created us to do. In the sweet, holy and mighty name of Jesus, Amen.

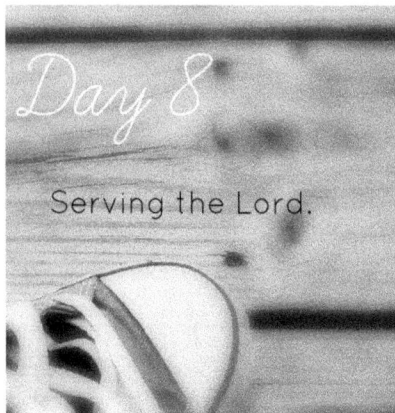

Day 8

Serving the Lord.

Scripture

Memorize today's scripture:

Serving the Lord (Romans 12:11).

You know the drill. We're wrapping up another verse in our passage today. Commit these three words to memory, write them on a note card and review!

Teaching

Serving is not natural. Whether we admit it or not, or are even conscious of it, we operate by the principle of numero uno: what's in it for me? Even when we do serve others, our motives can be selfish.

To serve the Lord is to yield to Him with such devotion that we ignore our own will, agenda and interests in order that He can use us to achieve His purposes. We become nothing; it's all about Him.

Like it or not, the essence of this life app is slavery:

> Do you not know that to whom you present yourselves slaves to obey, you are that one's slaves whom you obey, whether of sin leading to death, or of obedience leading to righteousness? (Romans 6:16).

Before we are saved, we don't have a choice of master. We are exclusively subject to the rule of sin. "But when the kindness and the love of God our Savior toward man appeared, not by works of righteousness which we have done, but according to His mercy He saved us, through the washing of regeneration and renewing of the Holy Spirit" (Titus 3:4-5). As a result, we are no longer slaves to sin (Romans 6:6)!

In the oxymoron of all times, bondage to Christ, even though we become His slave, is the only form of genuine freedom! "Therefore if the Son makes you free, you shall be free indeed" (John 8:36).

Saved by God's work in us, Paul explains, we must actively reject sin for righteousness:

> Do not let sin reign in your mortal body, that you should obey it in its lusts. And do not present your members as instruments of unrighteousness to sin, but present yourselves to God as being alive from the dead, and your members as instruments of righteousness to God (Romans 6:12-13).

We are confronted with the same ultimatum Joshua issues the Israelites once they settle in the Promised Land and the Lord gives them rest from their enemies: "Choose for yourselves this day whom you will serve" (Joshua 24:15).

It's a decision that necessitates an undivided heart: "No one can serve two masters; for either he will hate the one and love the other, or else he will be loyal to the one and despise the other" (Matthew 6:24).

There's no fence. It's one or the other. By not choosing, and riding the fence, we are still making a choice. What will yours be?

I side with Joshua, who emphatically declares in Joshua 24:15:

> As for me and my house, we will serve the Lord.

Once we decide to serve the Lord, what's next? Deuteronomy 10:12-13 answers:

> And now, Israel (or Shauna, or fill in your name here _____), what does the Lord your God require of you, but to fear the Lord your God, to walk in all His ways and to love Him, to serve the Lord your God with all your heart and with all your soul, and to keep the commandments of the Lord and His statutes which I command you today for your good (parentheses mine)?

As bondservants of Christ, we do "the will of God from the heart, with goodwill doing service, as to the Lord, and not to men" (Ephesians 6:6-7). Whatever we do, we do heartily, "as to the Lord and not to men, knowing that from the Lord you will receive the reward of the inheritance" (Colossians 3:23-24).

In our instant-gratification world, here's how to make the continual sacrifices servanthood requires for a payoff that is oftentimes eternal:

1. "In newness of the Spirit" (Romans 7:6), walking by the Spirit, and not fulfilling the lust of the flesh (Galatians 5:16), in "righteousness and peace and joy in the Holy Spirit. For he who serves Christ in these things is acceptable to God and approved by men" (Romans 14:18). (More on this on *Day 30*.)

2. With fear of the Lord and gladness, rejoicing with trembling, coming before His presence with singing (Psalm 2:11, 100:2).

3. Through suffering, "serving the Lord with all humility, with many tears and trials" (Acts 20:19).

4. Without distraction and for your own profit (1 Corinthians 7:35).

5. With perseverance, because even when we mess up, our sins don't nullify our ability to be used of God. "Do not fear. You have done all this wickedness; yet do not turn aside from following the LORD, but serve the LORD with all your heart" (1 Samuel 12:20).

The only way to walk the talk is as a servant of the Lord. Every other life app from Romans 12:9-21 hinges on our total surrender to Him, His will and His ways. No longer bound to sin, we can now serve the Lord in all things, fully pleasing Him, fervent in spirit, not lagging in diligence, giving preference to one another and kindly affectionate to one another with brotherly love.

Example

Let's develop a profile for a servant of the Lord. Look up the following scriptures in your Bible (NKJV if possible), and fill in the blanks below.

Profile of a Servant of the Lord

Joshua 24:14

1. _____ the Lord;

2. Serves in _____ and _____;

3. Puts away other _____.

1   Corinthians 4:1-2

4. Is a _____ of the mysteries of Christ;

5. Is found _____.

Colossians 3:12-17

1. Puts on tender _____, _____, _____,

   _____, and _____;

2. _____ with one another;

3. _____ one another;

4. Puts on _____, which is the bond of perfection;

5. Lets the _____ of God _____ in his heart;

6. Is _____;

7. Lets the _____ of Christ dwell in him _____.

8. Does everything in the name of the _____ _____.

2 Timothy 2:3

9. Endures _____ as a _____ of Jesus Christ.

2 Timothy 2:24-25

10. Does not _____;

11. Is _____ to all;

12. Is able to _____ ;

13. Is _____ ;

14. In humility _____ those who are in opposition.

Practice & Prayer

Have you made a choice as to whom you will serve as master? To serve anyone or anything but God, including ourselves, is idolatry. Will you serve idols or the one true living God? Talk about where you are with this decision.

_____

_____

_____

_____

Words have power. Proverbs 18:21 tells us life and death are in the power of the tongue. Using the profile from our *Example* today, insert your name and declare the characteristics of a servant for yourself out loud. For example, for Colossians 3:12-17, I would say:

__Shauna__ puts on tender mercies, kindness, humility, and meekness, and longsuffering. __Shauna__ bears with others. __Shauna__ forgives others. __Shauna__ puts on love, which is the bond of perfection. __Shauna__ lets the peace of God rule in her heart. __Shauna__ is thankful. __Shauna__ does everything in the name of the Lord Jesus.

Now you do it with your name, inserting yourself in your profile.

_____

_____

_____

_____

_____

What is the one characteristic you believe is most critical for you to learn or improve?

_____

Challenge for Today

Think of a specific way you can practice the one characteristic you named above TODAY. Write down your exact plan for carrying this out.

_____

_____

_____

Now do it, and afterwards, come back and write about it here. What did you do? How was it different than what you normally would have done in that same situation? What happened? How did you feel? What did you learn about yourself and/or being a servant? What do you think it will take to make this a lifestyle and not just a one-time challenge?

_____

_____

_____

_____

_____

Let's Pray: Lord, I thank You that no matter how we measure up to the profile of a servant, You have started a good work in us, and YOU are faithful to complete it. Help us today to surrender to You in all things that one day we would hear You say to us: "Well done, good and faithful servant." In the sweet, holy and mighty name of Jesus, Amen.

Day 9

Rejoicing in hope.

Scripture

Memorize today's scripture:

Rejoicing in hope (Romans 12:12).

Let's start a new verse today. Again, it's just three words! Commit them to memory, write out your index card and keep reviewing what you've already learned. You're doing great!

Teaching

Hope.

It is the anticipation or expectation of something good.

Like oxygen, we have to have it, because without it, we literally can lose our will to live, as tens of thousands of Americans do every year, taking their own lives because of despair so overwhelming death seems the only solution. The leading cause of suicide? Depression.

Maybe you've never experienced that degree of hopelessness (I hope you haven't and never will!), but you know well the heaviness of constant disappointment because something you desperately desire remains elusive.

I spent much of my life in this state: hinging my happiness on that someone or something I thought would make me happy. I set my eyes on the object of my desire, and it ruled my sense of well-being. As a young woman, I wanted to be tall, thin, fashionable, popular and noticed (okay, I still struggle with this one). In my career, I wanted the other person's position or account; I wanted more money or more recognition. As a new wife and mother, I wanted a lifestyle and possessions others had but were out of my reach. I wanted my husband to change and my marriage to be peaceful, and I wanted to stay home with my children. I wanted to be the sweet, serene, godly women I admired at church.

In the absence of what I thought would improve me or my lot in life, hopelessness found its home in my heart. I lived the reality of Proverbs 13:12: "Hope deferred makes the heart sick."

Everything that makes up our insides – our heart, soul, mind, will, character, emotions and even courage – becomes weak, wounded, grieved and tired when our hopes are dragged along and the realization of what we want so badly is drawn out or destroyed.

But there's another truth in this verse: "But then when the desire comes, it is a tree of life." When the longing of our heart comes to pass, we are revived!

The key to unwavering hope is the whom or what of our desire.

Today's life app is telling us to be exceedingly glad in joyful and confident anticipation of eternal salvation and in the One who is its very foundation!

If our hope is in other people or circumstances and the things of this world, "where moth and rust destroy and where thieves break in and steal" (Matthew 6:19), we will continually be vulnerable to disappointment and hopelessness. Every material item, fleshly pleasure, human hero or physical security we could possibly treasure here on this earth is subject to the here-today-gone-tomorrow threat, including our very life.

Not only that, Colossians 2:8 warns, "Beware lest anyone cheat you through philosophy and empty deceit, according to the tradition of men, according to the basic principles of the world, and not according to Christ."

Everything the world throws at us – including its wisdom, reasoning and ways – is a cheap imitation of the hope only Jesus can bring; empty lies that lead to one common destination: hopelessness!

However, if the object of our hope is the One who never leaves or forsakes us (Hebrews 13:5), the One who is the same yesterday, today and forever (Hebrews 13:8), the One whose blood saves us (Hebrews 10:19), the One through whom our salvation is guaranteed (Ephesians 1:13-14), the One from whom no one and nothing on this earth can separate us (Romans 8:38-39), and if the object of our hope is the expectation of eternal life with Him, then we're NEVER without hope and always have reason to rejoice!

Even in the midst of tragedy. Even when we're struggling. Even when everything around us is hopeless, as Romans 5:1-5 explains:

> Having been justified by faith, we have peace with God through our Lord Jesus Christ, through whom also we have access by faith into this grace in which we stand, and **rejoice in hope** of the glory of God. And not only that, but we also glory in tribulations, knowing that tribulation produces perseverance; and perseverance, character; and character, hope. Now **hope does not disappoint**, because the love of God has been poured out in our hearts by the Holy Spirit who was given to us (emphasis mine).

Hope in Jesus never disappoints. Not now. Not ever.

This is not the end, "for surely there is a hereafter, and your hope will not be cut off" (Proverbs 23:18). In Christ, we are assured eternity with Him, "which God, who cannot lie, promised before time began" (Titus 1:2). We have been sealed and given the Holy Spirit as a guarantee (2 Corinthians 1:21-22).

An eternal perspective enables us to endure, for "if we hope for what we do not see, we eagerly wait for it with perseverance" (Romans 8:25). And so Paul writes in 2 Corinthians 4:16-18:

> Therefore we do not lose heart. Even though our outward man is perishing, yet the inward man is being renewed day by day. For our light affliction, which is but for a moment, is working for us a far more exceeding and eternal weight of glory, while we do not look at the things which are seen, but at the things which are not seen. For the things which are seen are temporary, but the things which are not seen are eternal.

That is why Jesus continues to say in Matthew 6:20-21, "Lay up for yourselves treasures in heaven, where neither moth nor rust destroys and where thieves do not break in and steal. For where your treasure is, there your heart will be also." Where our treasure is, there will be our desires and affections. Our hope.

When our eyes are fixed on Jesus, rejoicing naturally follows, sometimes as an emotional response, but many times as a heart attitude we choose based on the word of God as it reveals His character and assurances.

Example

Look up the followings scriptures and fill in the blanks to see what else the Bible teaches us about hope.

1. We hope in God's _____ (Psalm 119:81, Psalm 130:5).

2. _____ is he whose hope is in the LORD his God (Psalm 146:5).

3. Through the patience and comfort of the _____ we have hope (Romans 15:4).

4. By the _____ we eagerly wait for the hope of righteousness by faith (Galatians 5:5).

5. Our hope is laid up for us in _____ (Colossians 1:5).

6. We must be grounded and steadfast in faith, not moved away from the hope of the _____

    (Colossians 1:23).

7. The hope of salvation is a _____ (1 Thessalonians 5:8); the purpose of a helmet

    is to protect our minds!

8. We must hold fast the confidence and the rejoicing of hope _____ to the _____

    (Hebrews 3:6).

9. This hope we have is an _____ of the soul, both _____ and _____

    (Hebrews 6:19).

Practice & Prayer

Being painfully honest, name any counterfeits in which you tend to place your hope – people, circumstances, positions, possessions, achievements, relationships, etc. you fix your mind on because you think it will make you happy. What usually happens? Are you left completely satisfied, not wanting anything more, or does the nagging need for something else remain? Write your thoughts here.

_____

_____

_____

_____

_____

How do you normally handle feelings of hopelessness? Where do you turn or what do you do?

_____

_____

_____

What is the main interference to anchoring your hope in Jesus and the promise of eternal life?

_____

_____

_____

Challenge for Today

You've heard the saying, "The grass is always greener on the other side of the fence." I have a saying of my own: Gratitude grows green grass. Rejoice in hope as a heart attitude you choose today. Second Corinthians 10:5 tells us to take captive every thought and make it obedient to Christ, whose word tells us to give thanks always for *all things* (Ephesians 5:20). Make the choice to rejoice!

Sometimes we just need to STOP:

> **S**eek the Lord
> **T**ell Him my temptation
> **O**pen my heart to His redirection (another way of saying be willing to repent!)
> **P**urpose to do what He desires

Grab a 3x5 card, and on one side, write the main interference or counterfeit that keeps you from anchoring your hope in Jesus, and below it, copy the acronym for STOP.

Now, choose three assurances from the list you completed in our *Example* section today that will help you when you find yourself misplacing your hope. Copy them on the back of your 3x5 card and keep it with you everywhere you go today. When hopelessness or even a tinge of discontentment threatens, STOP. Literally, pause whatever you're doing and give turn your attention to the Lord. Take a moment to tell Him your temptation and then praise Him for His assurances, out loud if at all possible and repeatedly if necessary. For example, you might say something like:

> Lord, right now, as I think about/am confronted with _____,
> I rejoice because my hope is laid up for me in heaven. My name is written in heaven!
> Thank You that I am grounded and steadfast in faith and will not be moved away from
> the hope of the gospel. Thank You that the hope I have in You is the anchor of my soul,
> sure and steadfast, and the helmet for my mind. I rejoice, Lord, I rejoice!

Tell Him you are willing that He would redirect your heart and mindsets according to His will, and make the decision to do what pleases Him.

At the end of the day, write down what happened. How did choosing to rejoice change your mindset in the moment? Did you have to practice more than once? Did it get easier? Do you see the value in making this a daily, lifelong habit?

_____

_____

_____

Let's Pray: Lord, thank You that Your thoughts toward us are of peace, to give us a future and a hope (Jeremiah 29:11). We place our hope in Jesus Christ and Your promise of eternal salvation. You are the God of hope, and our hope is in You! Give us the spirit of wisdom and revelation in the knowledge of You, the eyes of our understanding being enlightened; that we may know what is the hope of Your calling, what are the riches of the glory of Your inheritance in the saints, and what is the exceeding greatness of Your power toward us who believe (Ephesians 1:17-19). Please fill us with all joy and peace in believing that we may abound in hope by the power of the Holy Spirit (Romans 15:13). In the sweet, holy and mighty name of Jesus, Amen.

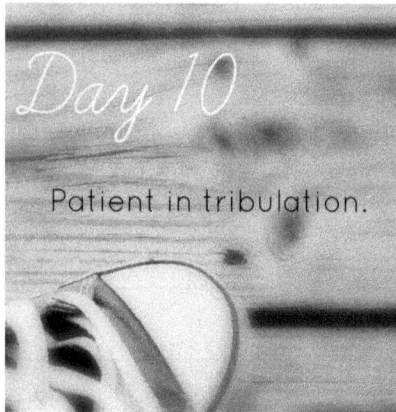

Day 10

Patient in tribulation.

Scripture

Memorize today's scripture:

Patient in tribulation (Romans 12:12).

Once again, we have just three words to commit to memory. You can do it! Add these to your index card, commit them to memory, and then review what you've mastered so far. How are you doing with the entire passage? Spend some extra time on it if you're lagging a bit behind.

Teaching

Tribulation is one of those topics most of us would rather avoid. Who wants to think about oppression, affliction and distress? Unfortunately or maybe fortunately (as we'll see shortly), it is a fact of life, and especially for followers of Jesus Christ, who tells us in John 16:33:

> These things I have spoken to you, that in Me you may have peace. In the world you will have tribulation; but be of good cheer, I have overcome the world.

It's not *if* we will have tribulation, it's *when*, and today's life app answers the what to do of the when we do: be patient. In the Greek, it means to bravely and calmly hold fast to our faith in the face of trials, misfortune, cruelty and hardship.

It follows rejoicing in hope because our hope in Christ and the promise of eternal life with Him makes it possible to be patient in tribulation. Confident expectation enables us to stand firm in Christ regardless of what's happening in and around us.

When difficulties arise, to be patient is to resist the urge to flee. When misfortune strikes, to be patient is to trust God's sovereignty. When doubts assail us, to be patient is to refuse to leave the faith. When following Jesus results in rejection and ill treatment, to be patient is to abide in Him and obey. When hard times linger and we can't see an end in sight, to be patient is to fix our eyes on Jesus and trust that God is who He says He is and will do what He says He will do. When marriage gets challenging, to be patient is to stay put. (Please note, I am not talking about staying put if you or your children are in danger. Get to safety!)

The answer for how we do this is in the "these things" Jesus references in John 16:33 above, giving us a clue that we need to look in the preceding chapters and verses to find out what He's talking about. In John chapter thirteen, Jesus finishes the last supper with His disciples, confronts Peter's inevitable triple denial, and then explains to His disciples that He's not going to be around much longer. He lets them know they will see Him again, and then He goes on to tell them "these things."

When we stand firm on the truths below, "these things" become the source of the peace and good cheer that enable us to be patient in tribulation, that we should not stumble (John 16:1):

> Jesus is the way, the truth, and the life; we have access to God the Father through Him (14:6).

> We will do the same and greater works than He (14:12).

> Whatever we ask in Jesus' name, that He will do (14:13-14); whatever we ask the Father in His name, the Father will give us that our joy may be full (16:23-24).

> He will give us a Helper, the Holy Spirit, the Spirit of truth, to dwell with and in us forever (14:16-17, 16:7).

> The Holy Spirit will teach us all things and bring to mind the things Jesus has said (14:26), guiding us into all truth and telling us things to come (16:13).

> He will not leave us orphans, but will come to us (14:18).

> Because He lives, we will live also (14:19).

> Jesus will love us and manifest Himself to us (14:21).

> He will give us His peace that our hearts won't be troubled or afraid (14:27).

> His joy will remain in us that our joy may be full (15:11).

> Our sorrow will be turned into joy (16:20).

> Our hearts will rejoice and no one will be able to take our joy from us (16:22).

If God is willing to do all of this for us, why doesn't He just keep us from tough times and grief altogether? Why must we enter the kingdom of God through many tribulations (Acts 14:22)? What we must remember is that the here and now is not just about what's happening right in front of us; it's about what God is accomplishing in and through us and what's to come. Our confident expectation. The reason for our patience.

First Peter 1:6-9 explains:

> In this you greatly rejoice, though now for a little while, if need be, you have been grieved by various trials, that the genuineness of your faith, being much more precious than gold that perishes, though it is tested by fire, may be found to praise, honor, and glory at the revelation of Jesus Christ, whom having not seen you love. Though now you do not see Him, yet believing, you rejoice with joy inexpressible and full of glory, receiving the end of your faith—the salvation of your souls.

Jesus has overcome the world and everything in it, including tribulation. We can have peace – we can be patient and stick out our faith in Christ – because Christ has overcome the world. He has already prevailed over any and all tribulation we may face! We are more than conquerors in Christ Jesus, and He "is able to do exceedingly abundantly above all that we ask or think, according to the power that works in us" (Ephesians 3:20).

No matter what God may ask or allow us to endure in our time here on earth, it will never be more than Christ Himself. More so, He endured the wrath of God due us. He didn't deserve the most gruesome, painful, humiliating death possible; we did. And yet now "His divine power has given to us all things that pertain to life and godliness" (2 Peter 1:3). We just have to stand resolute in faith, trusting God's promise to "supply all your need according to His riches in glory by Christ Jesus" (Philippians 4:19), remembering always, "I can do all things through Christ who strengthens me" (Philippians 4:13)!

Therefore, "count it all joy when you fall into various trials knowing that the testing of your faith produces patience. But let patience have its perfect work, that you may be perfect and complete, lacking nothing" (James 1:2-4).

Example

Scripture is full of examples of God's supernatural faithfulness to men and women who, even in the face of the most dire circumstances, are patient in tribulation, calmly and bravely holding fast to their faith. Unlike the superheroes of today, they don't have special or extraordinary superpowers. They are imperfect, scared and vulnerable just like you and me. They simply believe God and act on that belief; as they fix their eyes on Him, He demonstrates His supernatural ability to deliver. Many of their stories are recounted in Hebrews chapter eleven, which is sometimes called the "Hall of Faith." Read it once through in its entirety, and then answer the following questions.

1. How does verse one define faith? _____

    _____

2. What introductory phrase is used repeatedly throughout the chapter? _____

3. Read the chapter again, paying careful attention to what faith supplies or enables us to do. For example, verse two tells us that by faith we are able to understand the creation account, or in verse eleven, we see that by faith Sarah received strength. Name the five that speak most personally to you, completing the statement, "By faith, I…" Using our examples, you would write, "By faith I am able to understand creation," or "By faith I receive strength."

    (1) _____

    _____

    (2) _____

    _____

    (3) _____

    _____

    (4) _____

    _____

(5) _____

_____

4. What does verse six tell us about faith? _____

_____

5. Who does God reward? _____

6. Using any resource you have (*www.blueletterbible.org* is my favorite), look up the Greek meaning of *diligently seek*. Based on what you learn, what do you think it means to diligently seek God?

_____

_____

_____

Practice & Prayer

1. Going back to John, sandwiched in the midst of "these things" in chapters fourteen through sixteen, Jesus uses the illustration of a vine and its branches to instruct us in our part. What does John 15:4 tell us to do?

_____

2. Again, using any resource you have, look up the Greek meaning of *abide*. What does it mean?

_____

_____

_____

3. According to today's life app, what will it take to abide? _____

4. According to what we learned in Hebrews eleven, how will we be patient? _____

5. What relationship do you think abiding has to do with diligently seeking God? How might the two go hand-in-hand? What about by faith? What role does that have with diligently seeking God and abiding? Write your thoughts here.

_____

_____

_____

_____

Challenge for Today

By faith, as we are patient in tribulation, let us diligently seek God, investigating His faithfulness to others in order to build our faith. One of the ways we can do this is to read stories of martyrs and giants in the faith. There was a time when news of doom and gloom or stories of persecuted Christians would send me into a tailspin. As the Lord gives me understanding and eyes to see His goodness and faithfulness in all things, He strengthens my faith. Now stories of Christians standing firm in their faith in the face of unimaginable horrors are a tremendous source of encouragement that in Christ, I can too.

At the time of this writing, the shooting at Umpqua Community College in Roseburg, Oregon, just happened, leaving ten people dead. Survivors reported that the shooter singled out Christians willing to stand for Christ in the face of death. Kim Davis, the county clerk who refused to issue marriage certificates because of her religious convictions regarding homosexual marriage, was just released from jail. Bakers in Oregon closed their business and face $135,000 in fines for refusing to bake a cake for a homosexual wedding. We are going to need courage! We are going to need patience in tribulation.

Go online and find an organization that provides support, medical care, protection and/or financial assistance to persecuted Christians in nations where they are literally tortured for Christ (as of this writing, two such organizations are The Voice of the Martyrs and Open Doors). Scroll through their website for articles or stories, and spend some time reading about how Christians are being persecuted around the world. If the organization offers a way to get involved or write letters, do so!

Now, commit to regularly pray for one of the persecuted Christians you read about by name. Today's prayer is Hebrews 10:36-39, modified to give voice to our prayers for ourselves and our brethren:

Let's Pray: Lord, we have need of endurance, so that after we have done Your will, we will receive the promise: that Jesus will come and not tarry. Help us to live by faith. By Your Spirit, keep us from drawing back; rather, let us be of those who believe to the saving of the soul. In the sweet, holy and mighty name of Jesus, Amen.

Day 11

Continuing steadfastly in prayer.

Scripture

Memorize today's scripture:

Continuing steadfastly in prayer (Romans 12:12).

As you learn today's scripture, test yourself on verses nine through twelve. Make it your goal to master these four verses today.

Teaching

The Greek meaning of "continuing steadfastly in prayer," from the words *proskartereō* and *proseuchē* respectively, brings to mind images from an era when many households employed domestic staff. Undoubtedly, there were those who worked purely out of obligation, but there were also those who were steadfastly attentive to their employers from a place of loyal affection. They became like family, and out of love rendered unremitting care. Not only did they diligently attend to their duties, but they remained in a state of constant readiness to immediately answer a summons. They had already responded with their devotion before a need ever presented itself.

Likewise, to continue steadfastly in prayer is to be entirely dedicated and attentive to the Lord, constantly and persistently addressing our prayers to Him. Taking it a step further, it is abiding all the time in a place set apart for prayer – a state of constant and courageous readiness to pray because we've already responded with our devotion before the need for prayer ever presents itself.

While not exhaustive of all scriptures on prayer, the ones that contain the Greek word *proseuchē* provide insight as to what it means for us to continue steadfastly in prayer.

1. We are to emulate Jesus, who prayed for extended periods (Luke 6:12) and withdrew to pray in solitude (Luke 22:39, 41).

2. We are to pray as His disciples, who prayed in one accord (Acts 1:14), continuing "steadfastly in the apostles' doctrine and fellowship, in the breaking of bread, and in prayers" (Acts 2:42).

3. We are to "give ourselves continually to prayer and to the ministry of the word" (Acts 6:4).

4. Through the love of the Spirit, we are to strive together in prayer for each other without ceasing (Romans 1:9, 15:30), as the church did for Peter when he was in prison (Acts 12:5), "praying always with all prayer and supplication in the Spirit, being watchful to this end with all perseverance and supplication for all the saints" (Ephesians 6:18), laboring fervently in prayer

for one another that we "may stand perfect and complete in all the will of God" (Colossians 4:12), giving thanks as we mention one another in prayer (Ephesians 1:16, 1 Thessalonians 1:2, Philemon 1:4).

5. We are to ask from a place of believing (Matthew 21:22), anxious for nothing, making our requests known to God with vigilant thanksgiving (Philippians 4:6, Colossians 4:2) as "is the will of God in Christ Jesus for you" (1 Thessalonians 5:18).

6. We are to pray and fast (Matthew 17:21, 1 Corinthians 7:5).

7. We are to pray for the impossible, as did Elijah, who "prayed earnestly that it would not rain; and it did not rain on the land for three years and six months. And he prayed again, and the heaven gave rain, and the earth produced its fruit" (James 5:17-18).

8. We are to pray, trusting our prayers are heard and remembered in the sight of God (Acts 10:4, Acts 10:31).

These scriptures give excellent instruction for how and what to pray, but that's not all! I'm jumping up and down on the inside as I prepare to share what God revealed to me through the scriptures where *proseuchē* is used in relation to a "set apart" place of constant readiness!

What is that "set apart" place? As we learned on *Day 2*, it is the temple, once an actual building God established as His dwelling place, but now our very bodies. As His temple, or *oikos*, we are to be a house of prayer (Matthew 21:13a), praying without ceasing (1 Thessalonians 5:17). Just as a perpetual incense was required before the veil to the holy of holies in God's original tabernacle, our perpetual prayers are incense before Jesus in heaven (Revelation 5:8). In Revelation chapter eight, with the opening of the seventh seal, John sees an angel who's "given much incense, that he should offer it with the prayers of all the saints upon the golden alter which was before the throne. And the smoke of the incense, with the prayers of the saints, ascended before God from the angel's hand" (verses 3-4).

Do you see it? *WE* are the place set apart for prayer, and our prayers are offered upon the golden altar before the Lord's throne in heaven! Therefore, we are to be "sober and watch unto prayer" (1 Peter 4:7, KJV), keeping a check on our desires and impulses with a sound mind and calm temperament, because as we'll see next, bandits lurk in our hearts and minds to defile our temples.

Example

Remember our *Example* on *Day 2*, when Jesus cleansed the temple? Our temple becomes like the 33 A.D. den of thieves when bartering, idleness and the love of money steal our devotion and affections and interfere with our ability to stay in a "set apart" place where we can continue steadfastly in prayer and are ready at any time to respond to the Holy Spirit's call to prayer.

Let me give you an example of what that means. Sadly, it's a failure that moved me to a place of greater dedication and determination to remain in a state of constant readiness.

The very day I wrote the bulk of today's life app, I took a meal to a friend who had just been diagnosed with cancer. As we were curled up on the couch visiting, the Holy Spirit kept prompting me to lay hands on her and pray. "Yes, yes, I really want to do that," I would think. Then the conversation would turn. As I began to run out of time, her husband came home, and she excused herself to the other room. I had things I needed to get done at home, so I said goodbye and left. I never prayed.

Immediately I felt convicted, but instead of turning around and asking if I could pray with them before leaving, I got in my car and drove away.

What God showed me is that by elevating my personal agenda above God's agenda, I let a bandit invade my temple. I was not "ready" to respond to His call to prayer because my mind was occupied with the schedule I wanted to keep.

As He did in the temple in Jerusalem, we need Jesus to overturn and unseat anything we allow to rob Him of what is rightfully His. When Jesus cleansed the temple, "the blind and the lame came to Him in the temple, and He healed them" (Matthew 21:14). Jesus restored His temple to its God-given purpose and state, and then His work was done there.

When our temple is restored to its intended use, Jesus' work continues in and through us, as well. We become powerful praying saints through whom God's will is accomplished through prayer. When He prompts us to pray, we need to be ready and responsive. We don't even have to know why God is asking us to pray or what to pray, we just need to pray.

One year, while on vacation, I was snorkeling with my youngest daughter. One minute we were over deep water, and the next minute we were one foot above the coral reef. My daughter wanted to stand up, and when I urged her to keep floating to avoid cutting her legs on the coral, it spooked her. She started wailing uncontrollably, and I knew I had to help her back to shore. As I kicked like crazy, my mask fell off, and I struggled to keep her afloat and myself from drowning as we made our way back to safety. When I returned home, a friend of mine asked if anything was going on a certain day of our vacation, because the Lord had put me so heavily on her heart to pray. The day she mentioned was the day of this snorkeling incident.

I am so thankful she was obedient to pray! We may never know the effects of our prayers, but if the Holy Spirit urges us to pray, we can know He has a reason for it. If we are in that place of constant readiness, our temple can be used for its intended purpose.

Practice & Prayer

Are we, as God's temple, suited to the offering of prayer? Are our hearts pure and our minds uncluttered or are bandits plundering our devotion and robbing God? In the space below, identify any temple bandits God has revealed to you today. Who or what is distracting your heart and mind and diverting your attention from prayer?

_____

_____

_____

_____

_____

_____

_____

Challenge for Today

Today's challenge is two part.

1. Cleanse the temple.

   As Paul writes in 2 Timothy 2:22, it's time to flee youthful lusts and "pursue righteousness, faith, love, peace with those who call on the Lord out of a pure heart," cleansing "ourselves from all filthiness of the flesh and spirit, perfecting holiness in the fear of God" (2 Corinthians 7:1).

   James 5:16 tells us, "Confess your trespasses to one another, and pray for one another, that you may be healed. The effective, fervent prayer of a righteous man avails much." Think of someone you trust and confess your list from *Practice & Prayer* to them. Expose your temple bandits, and ask them to pray with and for you. In the same way, ask them if they have bandits in their temple, and pray with and for them.

2. Be set apart in constant readiness to pray.

   As the Lord brings you opportunities to pray, drop everything and do it. If you receive an email, text or Facebook message asking for prayer, stop everything and pray. You can even type your prayer back to that person. If you're talking to someone and the Holy Spirit begins to nudge you to pray, don't just say, "I'll pray for you." Pray with them at that very moment. It might be awkward or uncomfortable, but I challenge you to make your temple available for God's use, whatever He may ask of you in prayer today.

In one of my all-time favorite books, *Living a Prayerful Life*, Andrew Murray says our private prayer life "makes it possible for one to do what he could not do by himself – maintain fellowship with God and receive the desire and power that equip a person for walking with God."[4]

Prayer is central to our walking the talk!

Let's Pray: Lord, thank You for the beautiful privilege of communicating directly with You in our understanding and with the spirit. Help us to maintain the purpose of our temples by expelling all bandits today. May our effective, fervent prayers avail much for Your kingdom and according to Your will today. In the sweet, holy and mighty name of Jesus, Amen.

---

[4]Murray, Andrew. "Living a Prayerful Life." Bethany House Pub., Bloomington, Minnesota. 1983, 2002. P. 129.

Reflect & Review

Take a few minutes to look back through this week's challenges. Did you remember to write down what happened when you completed your challenges? Are there any you never got to or want to redo? Is there anything you want to make note of as a record of what you see the Lord doing or something you otherwise don't want to forget? Use this space for your thoughts.

_____

_____

_____

_____

_____

_____

_____

_____

I'd like to finish and/or repeat:

_____

_____

_____

_____

_____

_____

Week 3

The outward expression of the inside job: how we treat others.

Days 12-17

The Outward Expression of the Inside Job

This week we'll look at the _____ expression of our _____ heart attitudes – how we treat others, both inside and outside of the _____.

What we'll find this week is an _____/_____ rhythm of _____ living:

> We are to live generously with our hearts, with our homes, with our resources, caring
>
> for those in the family of God and _____ what God's given us to
>
> others, even _____ of the cross.

The Outward Expression of the Inside Job

Outwardly, we are to do good to and show love to _____, but inwardly, we are to be wise in who we allow _____ the most _____ places of our lives, where our thoughts, beliefs and decisions are _____. Either way, it is:

> _____ rather than demanding,
>
> _____ verses expecting,
>
> _____ verses hoarding,
>
> _____ verses self-preservation.

The bottom line is this: others will know we belong to Jesus by our love, and our _____ love for Jesus will show _____ by how we treat others.

Five Inward-Outward Rhythms of Generous Living

1. Inwardly, our hospitable _____ make us outwardly hospitable to others in our _____.

2. Inwardly, we are a _____ that takes care of its _____; outwardly, because of our generous living, God adds _____ to the church.

3. Outwardly, _____ of Jesus create the _____ need for the family of God to take care of its own.

4. Inwardly, Christ must _____ our hearts to His toward those who persecute us; even more, we must outwardly _____ His blessings for them.

5. Our actions as insiders in God's family impacts outsiders becoming _____ who   affect more outsiders. The goal is for the outside _____ of God's work on the inside to make an impression on those on the outside looking in.

God's Abundance to Make Us Like Jesus

The abundance of God _____ our needs.

When we don't _____ God and generously share what is His anyways, we give place to the devil to offer _____ to those who need the real deal.

God's ways are _____, and when we follow His ways, He is found _____ in every way.

When we do what God tells us to do, _____ shines as the answer to every need, eliminating the _____ of counterfeit saviors.

_____-_____ living = the _____ expression   of   our   inward transformation into the _____ of Jesus.

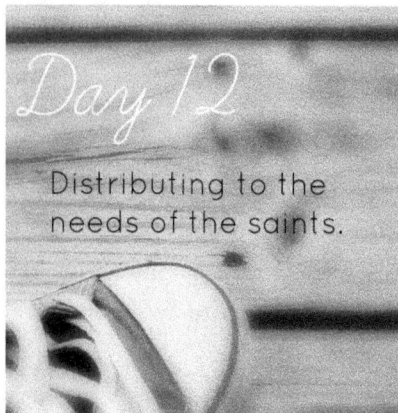

Day 12

Distributing to the needs of the saints.

Scripture

Memorize today's scripture:

Distributing to the needs of the saints (Romans 12:13).

How are you doing with so far? Today we begin our fifth verse. Commit this segment to memory, and then see if you can remember it along with verses nine through twelve.

Teaching

Today's and tomorrow's life apps have to do with how we treat others inside the body of Christ: our brethren or the saints.

Consider a business partnership. As a partner, you share in everything together. You set goals together, plan ways to reach those goals and work alongside one another to achieve them, doing whatever it takes. Each one has a stake, for themselves and on behalf of their partner(s). You sink or swim as a team. The more one is willing to invest in successfully achieving the partnership's goals, the greater the chance of success, and the greater the reward to all involved. All the resources of the partnership are available to advance it toward its defined end.

That's the picture Paul is painting in our life app today. When we think about distributing to the needs of the saints, we might automatically think only about handing out or supplying physical requirements like food, clothing, shelter and income. While that is part of it, the word *distributing* in the Greek, *koinōneō*, has a much deeper and broader meaning of partnering in the needs of the saints, joining in fellowship or communion with them and becoming their associates not just in supplying their lack, but in their kingdom duty or business.

It is a partnership among "those who are sanctified in Christ Jesus, called to be saints, with all who in every place call on the name of Jesus Christ our Lord" (1 Corinthians 1:2). That's us! When we are saved and sanctified in Christ Jesus, we are called to be saints! We are "no longer strangers and foreigners, but fellow citizens with the saints and members of the household of God" (Ephesians 2:19).

As such, we are to become associates in sharing the duties of a partnership in Christ Jesus to achieve His kingdom purposes for His church as a whole, even as He uses each one of us individually as a means to His end. "For God is not unjust to forget your work and labor of love which you have shown toward His name, in that you have ministered to the saints, and do minister" (Hebrews 6:10).

It's more than a financial alignment; it's a life alignment. It's not governed by a legal contract on paper; it's governed by God's grace at work in our hearts. It's not satisfied by a regular tithe check or the occasional special offering; it's sharing anything and everything we have because it's all His anyways.

It's a heart change followed by a new perspective that alters how we see everything we have and do: our time, our relationships, our families, our resources, our possessions, and yes, our finances.

After all, nothing is truly ours: "The earth is the LORD's, and all its fullness, the world and those who dwell therein" (Psalm 24:1, 50:12). He is allowed to interrupt us and access anything He's given us at anytime for whatever reason, whether we understand it, agree with it or see the reason for it:

> For by Him all things were created that are in heaven and that are on earth, visible and invisible, whether thrones or dominions or principalities or powers. All things were created through Him and for Him. And He is before all things, and in Him all things consist (Colossians 1:16-17).

This is one of those mindsets that clashes with culture's view to amass all you can, and if you have enough and some left over, then give. If you're able to satisfy your responsibilities and pleasures and can fit in some giving and serving, then by all means, do so, especially around the holidays.

Many times, giving our time and resources gains us an advantage, such as community service hours that look good on a resume, a tax deduction or the admiration of others. Sometimes we give as a means to gain recognition, for self-serving satisfaction or out of obligation, because we know it's what the Bible requires, such as tithes and offerings. Beware: the same right action can have a wrong motive behind it.

The thing about the partnership of distributing to the needs of the saints is that it's so much more! It's sharing ownership in the stake God gives us and opening our hearts and lives to become a part of what He's doing in and through them. In the same way, they are to be sharing a stake in what we're doing. It's all of us committing everything that is God's anyways to His access in accomplishing His work according to His economy.

Whatever holds us back is nothing compared to the abundance the Lord desires to pour out on those who give Him their all. We cannot out give God! Speaking of the tithe, I love Malachi 3:10, where the Lord actually says to try Him! He says, "'Bring all the tithes into the storehouse, that there may be food in My house, and try Me now in this,' says the LORD of hosts, 'If I will not open for you the windows of heaven and pour out for you such blessing that there will not be room enough to receive it.'"

We may not know exactly what form His blessings will take, but we can be sure they will be abundant. We can stake our partnership with the saints on the assurance we saw on *Day 7*: "God is able to make all grace abound toward you, that you, always having all sufficiency in all things, may have an abundance for every good work" (2 Corinthians 9:8).

Example

The ultimate example of this partnership among believers is found in Acts 4:32-35:

> Now the multitude of those who believed were of one heart and one soul; neither did anyone say that any of the things he possessed was his own, but they had all things in common. And with great power the apostles gave witness to the resurrection of the Lord Jesus. And great grace was upon them all. Nor was there anyone among them who lacked; for all who were possessors of lands or houses sold them, and brought the

proceeds of the things that were sold, and laid them at the apostles' feet; and they distributed to each as anyone had need.

It's not just about sharing possessions; it's about having a generous heart! Scripture speaks generously to this topic, but let's take a look at eight specific instructions God gives for distributing to the needs of the saints as partners in Christ. I encourage you to take the time to look up each scripture reference in its entirety.

Eight Instructions for Distributing to the Needs of the Saints

1. Freely give beyond your ability, even when you're hurting or have nothing (2 Corinthians 8:1-4).

2. As we saw on *Day 6*, give yourself first to the Lord, and then give what you have (2 Corinthians 8:5, 12-15).

3. Mercifully give to everyone who asks of you, even your enemies, without question or expectation of return and without judgment (Luke 6:30, 37).

4. Give in the measure you'd like to receive (Luke 6:38).

5. Give on earth because your hope is set on God (1 Timothy 6:17-19, ESV).

6. Give to bring joy to you and others (Hebrews 13:16-18).

7. Give to grow the kingdom (Acts 2:42-47).

8. Give cheerfully, for God supplies that which you give (2 Corinthians 9:6, 10-11).

Will we give Jesus all we have by holding everything loosely, allowing Him to shift His possessions and resources among His people as He sees fit?

Practice & Prayer

When we do for others, who are we really doing it for according to Matthew 25:35-46? _____

What does Acts 20:35 tell us about giving and receiving? _____

_____

Read Philippians 2:1-4. It's familiar to us already from *Day 1*, but let's look at it again in light of today's life app. What does verse three forbid?

_____

What does it tell us to do? _____

_____

What do Philippians 2:1-4 and Acts 20:35 have to do with one another? _____

_____

_____

What does Philippians 2:4 have to do with our life app of distributing to the needs of the saints?

_____

_____

Challenge for Today

Think of a fellow saint who needs a partner. Perhaps it's a friend who needs someone to come alongside them to face something challenging. Perhaps it's someone at church who's struggling to keep up with the demands of daily life, or maybe it's your pastor or a missionary who needs prayer, time or financial support. Name them here:

_____

Ask the Lord to show you exactly what you can do to partner with that person. Write down what He shows you.

_____

_____

_____

Identify anything that holds you back. Write a prayer to God in the space below, confessing what holds you back and giving it to the Lord. Ask Him to radically change your heart and mindset in order that you would be able to lay all you are and have at His feet for His use.

_____

_____

_____

_____

_____

Let's Pray: Lord, everything we have is Yours. Thank You that even though You don't need us, You use us. Nothing You could ever ask us is more than what You asked of Your own Son. Give us strength through Your Holy Spirit to give all we have to all You desire to accomplish in and through us for the benefit of others and Your kingdom. In the sweet, holy and mighty name of Jesus, Amen.

Day 13

Given to hospitality.

Scripture

Memorize today's scripture:

Given to hospitality (Romans 12:13).

This completes another verse, so see how well you know verses nine through thirteen. Have someone drill you. Keep up with this each day, and soon you'll know the entire passage!

Teaching

I love to open my home to others. Whether it's one friend, another family, the youth from our church or a huge party – big and small, I love it all! From planning to shopping, cleaning (okay, my kids do most of this), cooking and making everything look special, I sincerely enjoy creating a warm and memorable environment where others can relax and enjoy being served. Even when kids are running everywhere, friendships are started and deepened and ministry occurs. Someone shares a struggle or need, and someone else encourages. People stop to pray for one another. Even as we spend our very last ounce of energy cleaning up, the sweetness of the fellowship lingers.

That's what I think of when I encounter the word *hospitality*, but what Paul refers to in today's life app is so much more than being the hostess with the mostess. As with many of our previous life apps, this one, too, is an intentional mindset of earnestly putting forth the effort to love and provide for the needs of other believers, those we know and those we don't, welcoming all with friendliness and generosity.

It is to receive a person as a companion, into compassion and care, extending a warm welcome as we grant them access to our hearts because we have wholly given ourselves first to God. We do it as if for Jesus Christ Himself, as He explains in Matthew 25:35, "For I was hungry and you gave Me food; I was thirsty and you gave Me drink; I was a stranger and you took Me in."

According to the Greek word Jesus uses for *stranger*, this person might be a foreigner from another country or simply someone who is foreign or alien to us, or it might be a new and unheard of person outside our family or circle of friends, but in the context of today's life app, it will be a believer.

The thing is, we simply don't know who that person might be, as we learn from the only other scripture that uses today's Greek word for *hospitality*: "Let brotherly love continue. Do not forget to entertain strangers, for by so doing some have unwittingly entertained angels" (Hebrews 13:1-2).

Being given to hospitality is an opportunity to put *Day 4*'s life app into practice and "be kindly affectionate to one another with brotherly love." It is remaining alert and attentive to all whom God

84

sends and extending gentle, family-type love even to those whose true identity might be hidden from us. We are to receive them as guests, astonishing them with our kindness, because that very person may have been sent by God. Paul experienced this hospitality, recalling in his letter to the Galatians, "You received me as an angel of God, even as Christ Jesus" (Galatians 4:14).

Stranger or not, in the context of today's life app, there is one thing we will definitely share in common, and that is faith in the undefiled gospel of Jesus Christ. In fact, sometimes it is necessary to refuse hospitality to one who is known to be an enemy of God and a threat to the gospel. Remember, yesterday's and today's life apps have to do with who we let in to the intimate places of our lives in such a way that they have influence over our thoughts, beliefs and actions.

Second John 1:10-11 warns, "If anyone comes to you and **does not bring this doctrine**, do not receive him into your house nor greet him; for he who greets him shares in his evil deeds." Likewise, Romans 16:17-18 cautions, "Now I urge you, brethren, note **those who cause divisions and offenses**, contrary to the doctrine which you learned, and avoid them. For those who are such do not serve our Lord Jesus Christ, but their own belly, and **by smooth words and flattering speech deceive the hearts of the simple**." In fact, 2 Thessalonians 3:6 and 14 instruct us to "withdraw from every brother who **walks disorderly and not according to the tradition which he received from us**...If anyone does not obey our word in this epistle, note that person and do not keep company with him, that he may be ashamed." (All emphasis added.)

While these scriptures seem harsh and contrary to loving others, they are God's love to His people as He is protecting us against those described therein, and if we're parents, our children. At the same time, it's important to remember we all were once strangers, "without Christ, being aliens from the commonwealth of Israel and strangers from the covenants of promise, having no hope and without God in the world" (Ephesians 2:12). It's not that we never have someone in our home who isn't a follower of Christ, but we do want to pay attention to the perimeters God gives us in His word and be cautious about how often and how long they stay and get comfortable in our hearts if they are not seeking Jesus and/or drawing us nearer to Him. We don't outright reject every single person because they don't profess Jesus as Lord, but we must have wise boundaries.

As for the brethren, when Jesus saves us, we have the responsibility to spread the gospel and encourage His church. Whether we are the ones to go or the ones to care for those who do:

> Do faithfully whatever you do for the brethren and for strangers, who have borne witness of your love before the church. If you send them forward on their journey in a manner worthy of God, you will do well, because they went forth for His name's sake, taking nothing from the Gentiles. We therefore ought to receive such, that we may become fellow workers for the truth (3 John 1:5-8).

As each one of us is given the responsibility to go and make disciples, every one of us is on assignment. In that sense, everywhere we go, when we encounter other believers, we should be given to hospitality.

"Therefore, as we have opportunity, let us do good to all, especially to those who are of the household of faith" (Galatians 6:10). Because this is how others will know we're Jesus' disciples.

If heaven had a Martha Stewart of hospitality, it would be Jesus, who tells us:

> In My Father's house are many mansions; if it were not so, I would have told you. I go to prepare a place for you. And if I go and prepare a place for you, I will come again and receive you to Myself; that where I am, there you may be also" (John 14:2-3).

Hospitality is preparing a place for someone else, whether heart, home or in Jesus' case, heaven! Look up the following scriptures and note what they tell us about how we should approach being hospitable.

Luke 19:5-6 _____

Acts 28:7 _____

Romans 16:2 _____

Philippians 2:29 _____

1 Peter 4:9 _____

3 John 1:5-8 _____

When Paul tells us to "be hospitable to one another without grumbling," that means we are not to murmur, mutter or secretly harbor displeasure. In the same way, what do you learn from Colossians 3:23-24?

_____

_____

According to 1 Thessalonians 5:16-18, what three things can we do to make sure we maintain a right heart attitude before the Lord?

1. _____

2. _____

3. _____

How do you think practicing these three habits helps to be hospitable?

_____

_____

_____

_____

_____

Practice & Prayer

Regardless of our age or stage in life, we can be given to hospitality to anyone, anywhere because it starts in our hearts with a readiness to respond to any request the Lord may present to us, sharing whatever He asks with whomever He asks because we truly believe all we are and have are the Lord's to use as He deems necessary (Romans 11:36).

We can be given to hospitality in our homes, for sure, but also in the lunchroom or common area at school or work, in the foyer, halls and classrooms at church, on ball fields and in bleachers, in the mall and at the grocery store. In fact, we can extend a warm welcome to whomever God sends our way wherever we are, receiving "one another, just as Christ also received us, to the glory of God" (Romans 15:7). In other words, we are to receive others mutually and reciprocally, the same way Christ received us, demonstrating His love for us. We can open our hearts to others for the purpose of sharing the love of Jesus Christ with them.

Challenge for Today

Take a minute to write about your heart attitude toward hospitality. In the NASB, our life app says, "practicing hospitality." Does it come naturally to you, or is it something you have to practice? Are you given to hospitality, or do you wait for others to extend a hand of friendship or make sure you feel welcome first? When the Lord asks you to make yourself vulnerable in order to share His love with others, are you quick to say yes, or do you secretly grumble and complain? If you live at home with your parents, what do you do to make guests in your home feel welcome, whether you want them there or not or whether you feel you can make a difference or not?

_____

_____

_____

_____

_____

Wherever you go, are you absorbed in your own agenda or are you looking for opportunities to touch others with the love of Christ?

_____

_____

_____

Ask the Lord to open your eyes to the people He wants to impact through you today. Everywhere you go, make a conscious effort to notice those around you and extend a warm welcome to someone, even if you feel or look foolish. I'm not saying to make a scene, but smile, say "Hello," give them a compliment or ask them about their day. It's not so much what you do or say as it is the desire to love them like Christ, because you love and want to glorify Him.

Write down what happens here. Who did you encounter and where? What did you do to be given to hospitality? How did you feel? How did the other person respond? What would you do different?

_____

_____

_____

_____

_____

Let's Pray: Lord, help us to be vulnerable with our hearts, our homes and our time. Thank You for going before us to prepare a place for us, the ultimate expression of hospitality. In our time here on earth, use us to welcome others as an expression of our love for You and Your love for them. In the sweet, holy and mighty name of Jesus, Amen.

Day 14

Bless those who persecute you.

Scripture

Memorize today's scripture:

Bless those who persecute you (Romans 12:14).

We're starting on a new verse today. Persevere! Write out your index card and review, review, review!

Teaching

People like their comfort zones, and there's really no way to come to Jesus or follow Him while remaining there.

Jesus is "a stumbling stone and rock of offense" (Romans 9:33). The cross is offensive (Galatians 5:11). It challenges man's pride, traditions and long-held beliefs. It confronts our sin, desperate condition and need for a savior. It strips us of any illusion of self-reliance and control and causes us to completely surrender to a God we can't touch or see with our human eyes. We have to completely depend on Him and do things His way rather than ours or the world's.

When we do, persecution will come. Today's and tomorrow's life apps deal with our outward response when it does, for 2 Timothy 3:12 warns, "...all who desire to live godly in Christ Jesus will suffer persecution."

Jesus explains why:

> If the world hates you, you know that it hated Me before it hated you. If you were of the world, the world would love its own. Yet because you are not of the world, but I chose you out of the world, therefore the world hates you. Remember the word that I said to you, "A servant is not greater than his master." If they persecuted Me, they will also persecute you. If they kept My word, they will keep yours also. But all these things they will do to you for My name's sake, because they don't know Him who sent Me (John 15:18-21).

The Greek word for *persecute* in today's life app, *diōkō*, embodies the idea of pursuing. In the connotation we most commonly apply, it is to pursue in order to cause trouble for someone – to drive them away, shut them up or shut them out. But it also means to eagerly pursue or intensely strive to acquire, as used in scriptures that instruct us to pursue the things of God.

As we *diōkō*, we face *diōkō*. And when we do, we'd better *diōkō*!

When we follow Jesus, the light of the world, we have the light of life. We no longer abide in darkness (John 12:46) but are "a light to those who are in darkness" (Romans 2:19), walking as children of light. As such, we pursue those things we named in *Day 3*'s example: peace, justice, mercy, humility, love, spiritual gifts, righteousness, godliness, faith, patience, gentleness, holiness and eternal life.

As we do and His righteousness in us confronts unrighteousness, light exposes darkness, and darkness does not comprehend light (John 1:5). Men love darkness, rather than light, because their deeds are evil (John 3:19), "for everyone practicing evil hates the light and does not come to the light, lest his deeds should be exposed" (verse 20).

People living in darkness will naturally resist the light; persecution will naturally follow.

As the Bible so often does, it instructs us to handle persecution in a way that is totally against our human nature. To speak God's protection, prosperity, joy, blessings and divine favor upon those who mistreat, reject, ridicule, ostracize, threaten, injure, destroy and otherwise pursue us in a hostile manner seems an impossible if not absurd response. Yet as followers of Christ, we can expect to be treated as He was, and we must also do as He did.

Ironically, as we bless those who persecute us, we're the ones who receive blessings! The suffering they inflict is the catalyst for our heavenly rewards! By faith, we are cashing in on the promise Jesus made to His followers in Matthew 5:10-12:

> Blessed are those who are persecuted for righteousness' sake, for theirs is the kingdom of heaven. Blessed are you when they revile and persecute you, and say all kinds of evil against you falsely for My sake. Rejoice and be exceedingly glad, for great is your reward in heaven, for so they persecuted the prophets who were before you.

The blessings should not become a self-serving motive for obeying Jesus, but we can know that our obedience always serves a larger purpose to glorify God. Therefore:

> Do not think it strange concerning the fiery trial which is to try you, as though some strange thing happened to you; but rejoice to the extent that you partake of Christ's sufferings, that when His glory is revealed, you may also be glad with exceeding joy. If you are reproached for the name of Christ, blessed are you, for the Spirit of glory and of God rests upon you. On their part He is blasphemed, but on your part He is glorified (1 Peter 4:12-14).

Let us do as Paul did, and *diōkō* "toward the goal for the prize of the upward call of God in Christ Jesus" (Philippians 3:14).

Example

Jesus sets the ultimate example of blessing those who persecute us as He shares the Last Supper with His disciples. We first encountered the scene on *Day 10*, and after today, we'll visit the Last Supper one more time on *Day 30*. For today, it's the setting where Jesus blesses His body to give to His disciples, even though He knows one will betray and begin the chain of events leading to His death on the cross:

> And as they were eating, Jesus took bread, blessed and broke it, and gave it to the disciples and said, 'Take, eat; this is My body'" (Matthew 26:26).

Jesus blesses the very body that would soon suffer the most gruesome punishment known to man in order to bring about the forgiveness of our sin and our salvation. Then, as He hangs on the cross, unjustly accused, tortured, ridiculed, humiliated, beaten and dying at the hands of those who persecuted Him, He prays, "Father forgive them for they know not what they do" (Luke 23:34).

His concern is their forgiveness. Still is. Perhaps blessing those who persecute us as Jesus did is for the same purpose: for the forgiveness of those who know not what they do. We cannot expect those who do not know Jesus or have the Holy Spirit as their Helper to act as if they do, yet isn't that what we find ourselves doing?

As followers of Christ, we exchange our lives for all of His – the happy and the good, as well as the sacrifice, suffering and persecution. Jesus blesses us in turning us away from our iniquities (Acts 3:26). Are we willing to be used by Him as He does the same for others, even those who persecute us?

Practice & Prayer

First Peter 3:14-18 starts with an assurance for us, saying, "Even if you should suffer for righteousness' sake, you are blessed." Look up the passage in the NKJV and write down what it tells us about facing persecution:

1. Do not be _____ of their threats (verse 14).

2. Do not be _____ (verse 14).

3. _____ the Lord God in your hearts (verse 15).

4. Always be ready to give a _____ to everyone who asks you a reason for the

    hope that is in you (verse 15).

5. Respond with _____ and _____ (verse 15).

6. Have a good _____ (verse 16).

What does the passage say will happen to those who confront us (verse 16)?

_____

What is the reason the passage gives us that Christ suffered for our sins (verse 18)?

_____

What could happen when we suffer for the unjust?

_____

Challenge for Today

Around the world, Christians are being imprisoned, tortured and killed for their unwavering faith in Christ. In the United States, a country founded on scriptural principles by men who sought freedom of religion and freedom of speech, Christians who hold to a strict biblical view of cultural and social issues are being persecuted and stripped of freedoms in schools, work places, politics and even their own homes and businesses.

As we desire to live godly in Christ, as we speak and stand for God's truth, we will face persecution. When we do, a good place to start blessing those who persecute us is to pray what Jesus prayed: Father, forgive them.

Is there someone who in some way, shape or form gives you a hard time for living righteously for Jesus? They treat you differently because they don't want or like the Jesus in you. It might be a friend, a family member, even your own children. Write their name(s) here:

_____

Inserting their name in each blank, pray for them right now and throughout the day. Every time you encounter persecution from this person, pray this blessing over them:

Lord, forgive _____ for they know not what he/she does.

Turn _____ away from his/her iniquities and protect _____.

Prosper _____.

Save _____ by grace through faith and fill him/her with joy in Your

presence. I pray for Your divine favor on _____.

May Your kingdom come and Your will be done for _____ on earth

as it is in heaven.

In Jesus' might name, amen.

Let's Pray: Lord, persecution is a beautiful thing as evidence of living godly in Christ. Let our lights shine brightly for You as You expose darkness around us and turn others away from their iniquities. Forgive our persecutors, Lord, and bless them. Help us to view our experiences in this temporary world with Your eternal perspective for Your glory. In the sweet, holy and mighty name of Jesus, Amen.

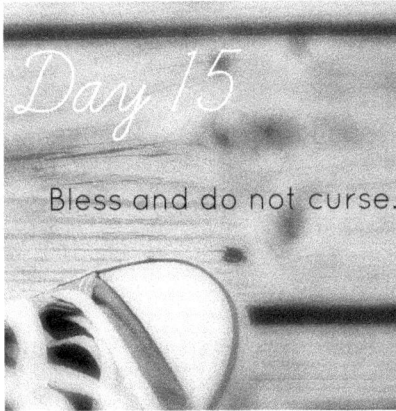

Day 15

Bless and do not curse.

Scripture

Memorize today's scripture:

Bless and do not curse (Romans 12:14).

This completes another verse, so add it to your stack of index cards, and see if you know the entire passage so far.

Teaching

I will never forget the last time I recklessly spewed hateful words at one of my children. It still knocks the wind out of me when I remember the look on my daughter's face as my curse left lips that should only carry blessings. The shock, hurt and sadness on her face as she stared at me in disbelief, tears welling in her eyes, betrayed the wound I inflicted. It doesn't matter that whatever she said or did was the last straw that day. I don't even remember the details of what I allowed to bring me to erupting.

No outside reason can excuse the inside source of my words, for "out of the abundance of the heart the mouth speaks" (Matthew 12:34). Clearly, my heart had a lot of anger that day, and my daughter was the casualty.

Have you ever said something you immediately wished you could retract? I've done so more times than I want to admit. Contrary to the age-old playground sing-song, "Sticks and stones can hurt my bones, but words will never hurt me," words hurt. Bad. We can never take them back, and as we learned on *Day 6,* one day every one of us will stand before God and give an account for every careless or idle word we've spoken.

Our words are serious business.

In the ten words that make up Romans 12:14, we encounter *bless* twice. That means it's significant, and today's life app juxtaposes speaking blessings with its antithesis: curses, which are spoken words that express our desire to see someone meet a disastrous fate, call down harm or speak evil against them.

In other words (no pun intended!), when we really want to say, "Sometimes I wish so-and-so would just _____ (you fill in the blank with whatever fate you'd like them to meet)," we need to zip it; and not only that, but speak the opposite!

As we learned on *Day 8*, we have a choice to either speak words that bring life or words that bring death; whichever we decide, our words will produce fruit, either juicy and delicious or stinky and rotting. Figuratively speaking, we will eat that fruit (Proverbs 18:21).

At first, we may have to force ourselves to speak words of life, and that's okay. Walking starts with baby steps. It's not about achieving perfection to please an unreasonable task master; it's about surrendering in absolute trust to a loving Savior whose wisdom directs us to what's best for us, others and His kingdom purposes. This is the heart of this study and my heart's desire for every one of us to truly grasp!

If you simply can't bring yourself to speak a blessing, then hold your tongue and pray: "Let my tongue cling to the roof of my mouth" (Psalm 137:6); "for there is not a word on my tongue, but behold, O LORD, You know it altogether" (Psalm 139:4).

As David proclaims in Psalm 39:1, let us guard against sinning with our mouths by restraining our mouths with a muzzles!

God knows our hearts, and He knows when the love of Christ compels us to do what pleases Him, but in our flesh, we struggle. As He sanctifies and transforms us, we can intentionally line our words up with His word. We can choose to "keep your tongue from evil, and your lips from speaking deceit" (Psalm 34:13), for "if anyone among you thinks he is religious, and does not bridle his tongue but deceives his own heart, this one's religion is useless" (James 1:26).

Example

Look at how James 3:2-8 describes our tongues:

> For we all stumble in many things. If anyone does not stumble in word, he is a perfect man, able also to bridle the whole body. Indeed, we put bits in horses' mouths that they may obey us, and we turn their whole body. Look also at ships: although they are so large and are driven by fierce winds, they are turned by a very small rudder wherever the pilot desires. Even so the tongue is a little member and boasts great things. See how great a forest a little fire kindles! And the tongue is a fire, a world of iniquity. The tongue is so set among our members that it defiles the whole body, and sets on fire the course of nature; and it is set on fire by hell. For every kind of beast and bird, of reptile and creature of the sea, is tamed and has been tamed by mankind. But no man can tame the tongue. It is an unruly evil, full of deadly poison.

He goes on to say:

> With (our tongue) we bless our God and Father, and with it we curse men, who have been made in the similitude of God. Out of the same mouth proceed blessing and cursing. My brethren, these things ought not to be so. Does a spring send forth fresh water and bitter from the same opening? Can a fig tree, my brethren, bear olives, or a grapevine bear figs? Thus no spring yields both salt water and fresh. Who is wise and understanding among you? Let him show by good conduct that his works are done in the meekness of wisdom (verses 9-13).

My friends, let us heed Paul's words in our walk with Christ today:

> Let no corrupt word proceed out of your mouth, but what is good for necessary edification, that it may impart grace to the hearers. And do not grieve the Holy Spirit of

God, by whom you were sealed for the day of redemption. Let all bitterness, wrath, anger, clamor, and evil speaking be put away from you, with all malice. And be kind to one another, tenderhearted, forgiving one another, even as God in Christ forgave you (Ephesians 4:29-32).

Practice & Prayer

What do you learn about the tongue from the following Proverbs? Fill in the blanks.

1. In the multitude of words _____ is not lacking, but he who _____ his lips

   is wise (Proverbs 10:19).

2. The mouth of the righteous brings forth _____ , but the perverse tongue will

   be _____ _____ (Proverbs 10:31).

3. There is one who speaks like the _____ of a sword, but the tongue of

   the _____ promotes _____ (Proverbs 12:18).

4. He who guards his mouth _____ his life, but he who opens wide his lips shall

   have _____ (Proverbs 13:3).

5. The tongue of the _____ uses knowledge rightly, but the mouth of _____ pours

   forth foolishness (Proverbs 15:2).

6. A _____ tongue is a tree of life, but perverseness in it _____

   the spirit (Proverbs 15:4).

7. Pleasant words are like a honeycomb, _____ to the soul and _____

   to the bones (Proverbs 16:24).

8. He who has knowledge _____ his words, and a man of _____

   is of a calm spirit. Even a fool is counted wise when he holds his _____; when

   he shuts his lips, he is considered _____ (Proverbs 17:27-28).

9. Whoever _____ his mouth and tongue keeps his soul from _____

   (Proverbs 21:23).

10. Do you see a man _____ in his words? There is more hope for a _____

    than for him (Proverbs 29:20).

Look back over the previous scriptures and list in chart form some of the blessings and consequences that result when are wise verses foolish, restrained versus loose with our tongues.

Wise Tongue _____   Foolish Tongue _____

(1) _____   _____

(2) _____   _____

(3) _____   _____

(4) _____   _____

(5) _____   _____

Can you think of a time when you've experienced either side of your chart? Talk about it here.

_____

_____

_____

_____

_____

Challenge for Today

Obviously, the Lord would have us bless with our tongues and not curse. But what if we don't even know where to begin, especially with someone we really want to curse? The best place to start is where we just came from: God's word! "My tongue shall speak of Your word, for all Your commandments are righteousness" (Psalm 119:172); "my tongue shall speak of Your righteousness and of Your praise all the day long" (Psalm 35:28).

If you can't think of a blessing on your own, speak God's word over the person you'd rather curse. Name them here (it might even be the person you named on *Day 14*).

_____

The Bible abounds with scriptures we can pray as blessings. I've listed a few of my favorites, modified into prayers for others. (Some of them might be familiar from other days, but let's look at them with fresh eyes as prayers of blessings today.)

Choose a blessing from the following list that you will intentionally speak to or over the person you named above today. Place a check in the box, and then insert their name in the blank(s). Continually declare God's word over them until you suddenly discover you no longer desire to curse them at all. You might want to write the blessing with their name on a 3x5 card and carry it with you until you find the Lord has changed your heart toward them.

- [ ] Lord, bless and keep _____; make Your face to shine upon _____, and be gracious to _____. Lift up your countenance upon _____, and give _____ peace (Numbers 6:24-26).

- [ ] Lord, give _____ the spirit of wisdom and revelation in the knowledge of Jesus Christ. Enlighten _____'s eyes of understanding that they may know what is the hope of Christ's calling, what are the riches of the glory of Christ's inheritance in the saints, and what is the exceeding greatness of Your power toward us who believe, according to the working of Your mighty power (Ephesians 1:17-19).

- [ ] Lord, according to the riches of Your glory, strengthen _____ with might through Your Spirit in _____'s inner man, that Christ may dwell in _____'s heart through faith; that _____, being rooted and grounded in love, may be able to comprehend with all the saints what is the width and length and depth and height – to know the love of Christ which passes knowledge; that _____ may be filled with Your fullness (Ephesians 3:16-19).

- [ ] Lord, may _____'s love abound still more and more in knowledge and all discernment, that _____ will approve the things that are excellent and be sincere and without offense till the day of Christ, being filled with the fruits of righteousness which are by Jesus Christ, to Your glory and praise (Philippians 1:9-11).

- [ ] Lord, may _____ be filled with the knowledge of Your will in all wisdom and spiritual understanding. May _____ walk worthy of You, Lord, fully pleasing You, being fruitful in every good work and increasing in knowledge of You. Strengthen _____ with all might, according to Your glorious power, for all patience and longsuffering with joy, giving thanks to You, Father, as You have qualified _____ to be a partaker of the inheritance of the saints in the light (Colossians 1:9-12).

- [ ] Lord, count _____ worthy of Your calling, and fulfill all the good pleasure of Your goodness and the work of faith with power, that the name of our Lord Jesus Christ may be glorified in _____, and _____ in You, according to Your grace and that of the Lord Jesus Christ (2 Thessalonians 1:11-12).

Let's Pray: Lord, as we have seen, there is not a word on our tongues that You don't know. "Let the words of my mouth and the meditation of my heart be acceptable in Your sight, O LORD, my strength and my Redeemer" (Psalm 19:14). "Set a guard, O LORD, over my mouth; keep watch over the door of my lips" (Psalm 141:3). In the sweet, holy and mighty name of Jesus, Amen.

Day 16

Rejoice with those who rejoice.

Scripture

Memorize today's scripture:

Rejoice with those who rejoice (Romans 12:15).

We're starting a new verse today, so go ahead and make another index card. Try reciting verses nine through fourteen from memory, and tack on today's life app. Keep at your scripture memory! Hiding God's word in our hearts is a powerful aspect of walking the talk.

Teaching

It's no accident that the Lord instructs us to rejoice in hope first (*Day 9*) before telling us to rejoice with those who rejoice. In order to be exceedingly glad with those who are exceedingly glad, as today's life app exhorts, our own happiness must be anchored in Christ alone.

What typically makes someone exceedingly glad? Usually, something incredible happens to them. They get the guy, or the new car, or the great job or the unexpected bonus. They get engaged or find out they're pregnant or they're expecting their first grandchild. They build your dream home or go on your dream vacation. They have the lifestyle or the body or possessions or pleasures that you want. Or maybe they experience a move of God or a healing you wish would happen to you or a loved one.

Our greatest obstacle to rejoicing with those who rejoice is likely to be jealousy and envy. Comparison and competition. The need to be better or have more or feel superior. Does anyone struggle with this?

Confession time, again. Once more, I'd rather not admit this, but I'm willing to be painfully honest and transparent with you if there's any chance it will encourage you to be painfully honest and transparent with the Lord.

Just yesterday, working through a Bible study I'm doing with my girlfriends, the lesson exposed a truth I've known but remanded to the recesses of my mind: I have a hard time relating to people if I don't know where I stand in comparison to them. In other words, if I conclude that somehow or in some way by the world's standards I'm superior to them (skinnier, happier, better marriage, better house, etc.), I'm at ease with them. Or conversely, if I'm clearly inferior (not as beautiful, not as thin, not as blessed, not as disciplined, not as accomplished, etc.), I may be discontent, but I know where I stand. If I don't, I'm unsettled at the thought of the person and how to relate to them. How's that for the ugly truth?

And here's why it matters: I will never genuinely be able to rejoice with others if I'm struggling with my own insecurity and discontentment because I'm always going to be comparing what they have or get to what I don't and coming up short. Viewing life through the lens of discontentment makes it difficult to recognize the abundance of blessings right before our eyes. Disappointment stealthily drags us into a state of despair, and it's hard to join a celebration with or for someone else when we're feeling sorry for ourselves. Ouch!

If our hearts are full and rejoicing in the hope of *Day 9*, we will be content and can rejoice with others. If we're jealous, bitter, discontent and ungrateful, we can't.

Paul describes his experience with contentment in Philippians 4:11-13:

> Not that I speak in regard to need, for I have learned in whatever state I am, to be content: I know how to be abased, and I know how to abound. Everywhere and in all things I have learned both to be full and to be hungry, both to abound and to suffer need. I can do all things through Christ who strengthens me.

Contentment is learned. It is not a natural state, but it can become the one that feels most natural to us through Christ who strengthens us. Hebrews 13:5 tells us why it's possible: "Let your conduct be without covetousness; be content with such things as you have. For He Himself has said, 'I will never leave you nor forsake you.'"

We can be content with exactly where we are, what we have and what He has us doing **because** He will never leave or forsake us. It's another shift in perspective. Another heart change. What do we hold most dear? If it is Jesus, we will always be abundantly satisfied. When we are satisfied, we can celebrate with others, even if they are receiving or experiencing something we'd like for ourselves.

When **who God is** becomes the source of our contentment, the only thing that matters and the only thing of eternal importance, gratitude naturally flows; but like contentment, we might have to be intentional about it before it becomes natural.

Regardless of where you stand today, know this: thankfulness douses discontentment. We can't be grateful and unhappy at the same time. We can't be grateful and angry. We can't be grateful and grumpy. We can't be grateful and resentful. We can't be grateful and envious.

The grass really isn't greener in someone else's pasture. There are brown patches, bald spots, chinch bugs, pits and burrs on both sides of every fence. Only God knows the side on which we belong. Trust Him. Thank Him. Let Him be the hope in which we rejoice, so we can rejoice with those who rejoice.

Example

Envy is a dangerous indulgence and the antithesis of rejoicing. Scripture speaks to the severity of this stronghold and provides numerous examples of how it leads to destruction and even death. Consider Cain, who killed Abel because God accepted his brother's sacrifice but rejected his (Genesis 4:2-8). Joseph's brothers hated him because his father loved him the most, and they sold him into slavery (Genesis 37:3-28). King David wanted another man's wife, so he had his way with her, and then he had her husband, Uriah, murdered in the front lines of battle (2 Samuel 11:1-17). The brother of the prodigal son couldn't celebrate the return of his wayward sibling because he was so worried about the injustice he perceived (Luke 15:11-32).

Envy is a work of darkness we are to cast off as we walk properly in Christ Jesus, making "no provision for the flesh, to fulfill its lusts" (Romans 13:12-14); it is a work of the flesh, not of the Holy Spirit (Galatians 5:19-23). It is "rottenness to the bones" (Proverbs 14:30) and a formidable foe.

James 3:14-16 warns, "If you have bitter envy and self-seeking in your hearts, do not boast and lie against the truth. This wisdom does not descend from above, but is earthly, sensual, demonic. For where envy and self-seeking exist, confusion and every evil thing are there."

Conversely, 1 Timothy 6:6-12 explains:

> Now godliness with contentment is great gain. For we brought nothing into this world, and it is certain we can carry nothing out. And having food and clothing, with these we shall be content. But those who desire to be rich fall into temptation and a snare, and into many foolish and harmful lusts which drown men in destruction and perdition. For the love of money is a root of all kinds of evil, for which some have strayed from the faith in their greediness, and pierced themselves through with many sorrows. But you, O man of God, flee these things and pursue righteousness, godliness, faith, love, patience, gentleness. Fight the good fight of faith, lay hold on eternal life, to which you were also called and have confessed the good confession in the presence of many witnesses.

Notice, Paul uses the word *fight*. We must contend with our envy and discontentment, struggle with the difficulties and dangers it presents and strive to gain ground toward greater faith. It takes effort to change course and chase after that which pleases God. Eternally, it is the only worthy fight.

Practice & Prayer

We become rejoicers when we're so content in Christ and trust Him so completely that we know in our knower that we have all He deems perfect for our lives; therefore, in our contentment, we can genuinely rejoice with those who rejoice. Our interest can be the best interest of others.

Starting today, we can practice these three simple steps to becoming a rejoicer.

Three Steps to Becoming a Rejoicer

1. Choose faith.

    As we've learned today, contentment is not accidentally discovered or acquired through osmosis. It is a conscious choice to renew our faith. Faith that above all, God is good; that our heavenly Father loves us and knows what's best for us. Faith that He is in control and does not allow what He does not intend to use for our usefulness to Him. Faith that He will direct our paths, directly or through those in authority over us, as we seek His will above all else.

2. Spend time praising God.

    When Jesus encountered the two Marys as they fled the empty tomb to report His resurrection to His disciples, Jesus commanded them in Matthew 28:9, "Rejoice!"

    What does the scripture say the women did? _____

    _____

    They worshiped Him! Rejoicing is worshiping God for who He is regardless of who we are or what's happening in our lives or the lives of others. It is beautiful (Psalm 33:1), and gratitude and contentment naturally follow.

What reasons does scripture give us to rejoice? Here are eighteen verses that speak powerfully to me. Look up all or some of them, but search at least five and note the reason each gives to rejoice!

Deuteronomy 26:11 _____

Psalms 5:11 _____ and _____

Psalms 13:5-6 _____ and _____

Psalms 31:7 _____, _____

and _____

Psalms 63:7 _____

and _____

Psalms 97:1 _____

Psalms 118:24 _____

Joel 2:21 _____

Luke 6:23 _____

Luke 10:20 _____

John 16:22 _____

and _____

Acts 5:41 _____

Acts 11:23 _____

Acts 15:30-31 _____

Romans 5:2 _____

and _____

Romans 5:11 _____

2 Corinthians 7:9 _____

Philippians 1:18 _____

The bottom line is this: There is always a reason to praise God, because three things never change – 1) who He says He is, 2) what He says He'll do, and 3) who He says we are in Christ Jesus. These things are certain and ALWAYS a reason for rejoicing!

3. Learn contentment.

   Repeat Steps 1 and 2.

Challenge for Today

Take a moment and make a gratitude list. In one column, write ten things about who God is. Write your own, or select ten reasons from the list of blanks you just completed. This is the list that never changes because who God is never changes; it might get longer, and I hope it does as you experience more of who He is, but you won't ever have to take anything off this list. It is the anchor for your gratitude. No matter what's happening, if you find yourself having a difficult time rejoicing, you can reference this list and begin praising God.

In the second column, showcase ten things specifically relating to you and your life for which you are thankful. Again, when you feel discontent, displeased, disappointed or otherwise bitter, come back to this list and recall God's goodness to you regardless of circumstances.

Who God is: What He's done for me:

1. _____   1. _____
2. _____   2. _____
3. _____   3. _____
4. _____   4. _____
5. _____   5. _____
6. _____   6. _____
7. _____   7. _____
8. _____   8. _____
9. _____   9. _____
10. _____   10. _____

Take a moment right now and praise God for the ten things He is and the ten things He's done for you. Make a choice to rejoice! Did praising God change your mindset? How?

_____

_____

_____

_____

Think of someone you know who is experiencing a time of rejoicing. Even if you don't "feel" the emotion of rejoicing for them, write their name below:

_____

Now call, text, email or mail them a note expressing your delight in what the Lord is doing for them. When you do, jot down what happened and how you felt:

_____

_____

_____

_____

Let's Pray: Lord, thank You for who You are and that we always have reason to praise You. Strengthen our faith, and by the power of the Holy Spirit, enable us to learn contentment. As Your children, help us to genuinely rejoice with those who rejoice. In the sweet, holy and mighty name of Jesus, Amen.

Day 17

And weep with those who weep.

Scripture

Memorize today's scripture:

And weep with those who weep (Romans 12:15).

Today's memory work completes another verse. Can you recite the seven verses we've learned so far?

Teaching

People who know me lovingly tease me about not being a crier. I have one friend I actually text from the movies if a tear escapes my eye because that's our measure for a genuine tear-jerker.

Even if I want to cry, most of the time I can't. Others don't want to, but can't stop. Perhaps it's part of our wiring or maybe our conditioning, but either way, the Bible is telling us as believers to weep with those who weep, whether we're criers or not. Because I'm not, I was extra curious as to why Paul gives this specific instruction.

The picture here isn't merely that of a heavy heart, concerned face and moist eyes as we nod our heads and speak words of understanding, encouragement or comfort. All that is good! I'm in no way minimizing any authentic display of sympathy.

But that's not the picture today's life app paints. Rather, it's wailing and howling and uncontrollably bawling – you know, the ugly, embarrassing kind of cry, either with the hurting or in a moment of our own privacy, because our hearts are truly broken for another.

The reason? Jump a few verses before of our Walk the Talk passage to Romans 12:5: "We, being many, are one body in Christ, and individually members of one another." This idea of being one body isn't new to us, right? We saw it on *Day 3* and *Day 4*, and we'll see it again on *Day 18*. If it bears repeating in scripture, it certainly bears repeating in our study!

With regards to weeping with those who weep, Paul teaches:

> For as the body is one and has many members, but all the members of that one body, being many, are one body, so also is Christ. For by one Spirit we were all baptized into one body – whether Jews or Greeks, whether slaves or free – and have all been made to drink into one Spirit. For in fact the body is not one member but many...that there should be no schism in the body, but that the members should have the same care for one another (1 Corinthians 12:12-14 and 25).

As one body, we weep with those who weep, because "if one member suffers, all the members suffer with it" (1 Corinthians 12:26).

Think of it this way. In the natural flesh, if I seriously injure or have a deadly infection in my leg, or worse, have a limb amputated, I will likely weep. A lot. If you are my leg or limb in Christ, I need to bawl if you are broken, hurting or separated. It is a matter of bearing one another's burdens and so fulfilling the law of Christ (Galatians 6:2), which is to love one another and thus be known as His.

We are one in the One, and as one, the One is glorified. Others will know the One by observing His body as one.

It is my genuine desire for God to break my heart with what breaks His and others'. I am not proud to tell you I can count on one hand the times I can remember weeping with those who weep, two of which were in the last year. I'm in my mid-forties.

One time, a new friend's husband was dying from cancer. She had become dear to me in a very short period of time, and she was so real and raw as she walked through his last days with him. My husband and I were out of town celebrating our anniversary as she spent her last days and hours with her husband in the hospital. Her pain and anguish broke my heart. I couldn't help but put myself in her shoes and found myself crumpled on the bathroom floor, weeping.

Another time, my daughter's heart was genuinely broken over deep disappointment. After holding her in my arms as she sobbed, I prayed for her, tucked her in for the night and then curled up in my own bed, weeping.

But it's not sorrow as if we have no hope (1 Thessalonians 4:13); rather, it's going before our Father in heaven, identifying with their suffering, pain or loss, and from our very depths, crying out to God for them. It's knowing that He's the one who knows the depths of their despair, and He's the only Balm that can heal their hurts. He is Hope itself.

It is there that we receive from Him what we need for others. He is "the Father of mercies and God of all comfort, who comforts us in all our tribulation, that we may be able to comfort those who are in any trouble, with the comfort with which we ourselves are comforted by God" (2 Corinthians 1:3-4), knowing that "weeping may endure for a night, but joy comes in the morning" (Psalms 30:5).

Example

James 5:11 describes God as "very compassionate and merciful." In the same way, we are instructed to "be kind to one another, tenderhearted, forgiving one another, even as God in Christ forgave you" (Ephesians 4:32). The word *tenderhearted* is the Greek word *eusplagchnos* from the root *splagchnon*, which is the same root word for *compassionate* in James 5:11 and literally means bowels or intestines or the seat of intense emotions like anger and love: our heart. It is the word used in Luke 7:13 when Jesus encounters the grieving widow who lost her only son and has compassion on her. He is moved as to His bowels! It breaks His heart.

So as God's chosen ones, we are to have a heart of mercy, one that is tender and breakable. It is actually something we put on like clothing (Colossians 3:12). We choose to sink into tender mercies, kindness, humility and meekness like we would put on an outfit.

In John 11:1-35, Jesus models weeping with those who weep. Fill in the blanks with what you learn from this story.

Jesus _____ Martha, her sister, and Lazarus (verse 5).

Jesus made it a priority to _____ where Lazarus was (verse 7), even though there was great risk in Him going to Judea (verse 8).

He gave Martha _____ (verse 23).

He redirected her focus back on _____ (verse 25).

He asked her, "Do you _____?" (verse 26).

When Jesus saw Mary, Martha's sister, and those who came to meet Jesus with her weeping,

"He _____ in the spirit and was _____" (verse 33).

Jesus _____ (verse 35) because He _____ Lazarus (verse 36).

Jesus was like us in every way (Hebrews 2:17). He was fully human and capable of deep grief and anguish. Jesus went to those who were hurting, was moved to tears because of their grief and wept with them. He is the example of what we should do, offering hope in Him as we share their sorrow.

Practice & Prayer

Do you have trouble weeping for others (circle your answer)?   Yes   No

Why do you think that's the case? _____

_____

_____

If you consider yourself a crier, would you say it's because that's how you're wired, or would you say it's because your heart literally breaks for others? Explain your answer.

_____

_____

If you're not a crier, what do you think is your greatest obstacle? Explain your answer. _____

_____

_____

Challenge for Today

Think of someone you know who is struggling or hurting. Write their name here: _____

Based on Jesus example in John 11:1-35, what would be your next step with that person?

1. Love them.
2. Go to them, even if it's troublesome.
3. Remind them of God's promises.
4. Redirect their focus to Jesus.
5. Give them hope.
6. Affirm and confirm their belief.
7. Groan in the spirit and be troubled for them.
8. Weep with them.

Write your next step here: _____.

Now take it, and jot down what happens. _____

_____

_____.

Let's Pray: Lord, break our hearts with what breaks Yours. Use us to weep with those who weep as one body in Christ, comforting them with the comfort we receive from You and witnessing Jesus. Thank You for Your Spirit within us and Your strength to bear one another's burdens, as if unto Christ Himself. May our compassion flow from hearts fully surrendered to You. In the sweet, holy and mighty name of Jesus, Amen.

Reflect & Review

Take a few minutes to look back through this week's challenges. Did you remember to write down what happened when you completed your challenges? Are there any you never got to or want to redo? Is there anything you want to make note of as a record of what you see the Lord doing or something you otherwise don't want to forget? Use this space for your thoughts.

_____

_____

_____

_____

_____

_____

_____

_____

I'd like to finish and/or repeat:

_____

_____

_____

_____

_____

_____

Week 4

Mindsets.

Days 18-21

Lesson Four

Mindsets

This week's homework focuses on our mindsets: our way of _____.

If something is wrong in the _____ of God's children, it will manifest in the _____ of Christ.

"For as (a man) _____ in his heart, so _____ he" (Proverbs 23:7).

> In Hebrew, *think* is *sha'ar* and *heart* is *nephesh*: Whatever we determine as true at the core of who we are on the inside is who we will be! It determines our walk.

The context of Proverbs 23:6-8 is _____ _____: a hypocrite can't fake who he is on the inside; our outsides _____ our insides every time!

The essence of this week's study is this: What we think is determined by what's in our _____; we are what we think as measured by what we _____.

We already know what's in our hearts is determined by Who is in our hearts, so in a way, Proverbs 23:7 encapsulates the _____ of our entire Walk the Talk passage:

We are in Christ and He is in us; _____ is what's in our heart.

Jesus _____ us determines what happens in our _____.

What happens in our _____ determines who we _____.

Who we _____ is measured by what we _____.

The mind and heart are connected: what is in our heart – _____ and our love for _____ – determines how we think and therefore _____ ourselves and others.

Having the Mind of Christ

When Paul talks about being of the same mind, he's not talking about brainwashing, but rather brain-_____. Not your mind matching mine, or mine yours, but both of us having the _____ of Christ. As our minds match that of Jesus, they will match each other, and therefore we will have the _____ _____!

Here's the progression to Paul's instruction in Romans 12:16 –

1. Be of the same mind: the mind of Christ.

2. Have the mind of Christ toward one another, as defined or expressed by:

   a. Mind not _____ _____.

   b. Associate with the _____.

   c. _____ humble.

Our culture may not look exactly like Rome in Paul's time, but there are still _____ that cause us to look condescendingly on others. However, the gospel _____ the   playing field on every account!

The Mind of Christ Is Humility

Each of us is redeemed solely by grace, and grace should produce one thing in us: _____.

And humility _____ the mind of Christ, as Paul writes in Philippians 2:3-8:

> Let nothing be done through selfish ambition or conceit, but in lowliness of mind let each esteem others better than himself. Let each of you look out not only for his own interests, but also for the interests of others. Let this mind be in you which was also in Christ Jesus, who, being in the form of God, did not consider it robbery to be equal with God, but made Himself of no reputation, taking the form of a bondservant, and coming in the likeness of men. And being found in appearance as a man, He humbled Himself and became obedient to the point of death, even the death of the cross.

The great _____ of this week's exhortation is _____. Mounce says:

> Like spokes in a wheel that converge at the hub, the closer we are to God the closer we come to one another. Paul admonished his readers not to be proud since it is pride more than anything else that destroys the _____ of the body.[5]

Pride has no _____ in our walk or talk. In humility, we must guard against high thoughts of ourselves or high things that take the high place that only Jesus should _____.

The mind of Christ determines the _____ through which we see others:

In Christ, who we are in our _____ or the eyes of the world is no big deal.

In the lowliness of humility there is no place

for making a _____ _____ of ourselves or others.

---

[5] Mounce, R. H. (1995). *Romans* (Vol. 27, p. 240). Nashville: Broadman & Holman Publishers.

Scripture

Memorize today's scripture:

> *Be of the same mind toward one another (Romans 12:16).*

We start working on another verse today. Learn these eight words, and then review. Were you able to recite it all together? Keep at it!

Teaching

My sister and I wasted our childhood fighting, the perfect example of the sibling rivalry we encountered on *Day 4*. Constant contentions pitted us against each other as we defended and advanced what we deemed rightfully ours – parental favor and attention, territory, property, privileges, chores (or the right NOT to have to do chores) and justice, to name a few things. As we looked out for number one, everyone suffered: we did, and so did our parents!

It's in our nature to take the "every man for himself" approach, but according to today's life app, God desires that we take an "every man for another" approach, giving our brothers and sisters in Christ the same consideration we would give ourselves. But before we can extend this same mind *toward* another, we have to possess the same mind, not in the sense of brainwashed robots, but as the collective body of Christ.

In the Greek, the *mind* of our life app is *phroneō,* which at an individual level refers to our understanding and wisdom, but also to how we feel and think, and our opinion of ourselves, especially that we "not let one's opinion (though just) of himself exceed the bounds of modesty."[6] At the same time, it embodies our tendency to strive for our own interests or advantage, like my sister and I did. Like we all do. In the public arena, it describes being on the same side of a party or issue as someone else.

In 1 Corinthians 2:16, Paul tells us "we have the mind of Christ." Here, the Greek word he uses for *mind* is *nous.* Like *phroneō, nous* refers to a person's intellectual ability to perceive, understand, feel, judge and determine, but also to "reason in the narrower sense, as the capacity for spiritual truth, the higher powers of the soul, the faculty of perceiving divine things, of recognizing goodness and of hating evil."[7]

---

[6] "Greek Lexicon :: G5426 (NKJV)." Blue Letter Bible. Sowing Circle. Web. 9 Jul, 2014.
<http://www.blueletterbible.org/lang/lexicon/lexicon.cfm?Strongs=G5426&t=NKJV>.
[7] "Greek Lexicon :: G3563 (NKJV)." Blue Letter Bible. Sowing Circle. Web. 11 Jul, 2014.
<http://www.blueletterbible.org/lang/lexicon/lexicon.cfm?Strongs=G3563&t=NKJV>.

When we have the same mind toward one another, our understanding and wisdom and the way we see ourselves and our interests will line up with Jesus' understanding and wisdom and the way He saw Himself and His interests. Because we have His mind, we have His ability to perceive and reason intellectually and spiritually; therefore, we will cherish what He cherishes, and in one accord, we will take one side: His. We will want what He wants, for ourselves, but also for others, and we will do what Jesus did.

What did Jesus do? What His Father told Him to do: "Most assuredly, I say to you, the Son can do nothing of Himself, but what He sees the Father do; for whatever He does, the Son also does in like manner" (John 5:19).

This is the mind we should have, saying and doing as the Father tells us in His word and by His Spirit; therefore, having the same mind toward one another. It's not adopting each other's views in order to agree with one another; it's together all moving toward God's view, and it's the only way that we, as the body of Christ, will be complete, equipped and prepared to be what God wants us to be and do what He wants us to do.

It's what Paul describes as being "perfectly joined together in the same mind and in the same judgment" (1 Corinthians 1:10). When our perceptions, feelings and opinions of ourselves and with regards to how things ought to be done are unified because they are the perceptions, feelings and opinions of Christ, then in one accord, as the body of Christ, we will be in right relationship to one another and can become what we ought to be.

Example

Right before Judas leads the detachment of troops to arrest Jesus for His trial and crucifixion, Jesus prays for His disciples. He knows He is sending them into a hostile world, and as we saw on *Day 3*, at the heart of His cry to the Father is unity.

His prayer in John 17:20-23 bears repeating here as it has to do with unity and us being of the same mind toward one another. He's not just praying for His disciples then, He's praying for us today!

> I do not pray for these alone, but also for **those who will believe** in Me through their word; that they all may be one, as You, Father, are in Me, and I in You; that they also may be one in Us, that the world may believe that You sent Me. And the glory which You gave Me I have given them, that they may be one just as We are one: I in them, and You in Me; that they may be made perfect in one, and that the world may know that You have sent Me, and have loved them as You have loved Me (emphasis mine).

When we have unity, the world knows Jesus, because they see His body edified and growing! It's part of the worthy calling from Ephesians 4:1-6 on *Day 4* when we looked at lack of unity as an enemy of the gospel.

In continuing his letter to the Ephesians, Paul explains that we are one body joined together by one Spirit with gifts and positions that all serve one purpose:

> ...for the equipping of the saints for the work of ministry, for the edifying of the body of Christ, till we all come to the unity of the faith and of the knowledge of the Son of God, to a perfect man, to the measure of the stature of the fullness of Christ; that we should no longer be children, tossed to and fro and carried about with every wind of doctrine, by the trickery of men, in the cunning craftiness of deceitful plotting, but, speaking the

truth in love, may grow up in all things into Him who is the head – Christ – from whom the whole body, joined and knit together by what every joint supplies, according to the effective working by which every part does its share, causes growth of the body for the edifying of itself in love (Ephesians 4:12-16).

Notice, we are to grow up in all things into Him who is the head – Christ. What's in the head? The mind! Unity happens when and because the body has the mind of Christ! It's the only way, because to have any other mind leads to self-seeking and division.

Practice & Prayer

So, how do we have the same mind toward one another? Paul goes on to tell the Ephesians to "put off, concerning your former conduct, the old man which grows corrupt according to the deceitful lusts, and be renewed in the spirit of your mind, and that you put on the new man which was created according to God, in true righteousness and holiness" (Ephesians 4:22-24).

The following scriptures instruct us in what to do on a daily basis in order to have the same mind toward one another. One is 1 Corinthians 4:6, which is familiar from *Day 7* and bears repeating here: "Do not think beyond what is written in the word of God, and do not be puffed up on behalf of one against the other."

Look the rest of these up and fill in the blanks:

1.   Romans 8:5 – Live according to the _____ and set your mind on the things of the

     _____.

2.   Philippians 4:8 – Meditate or think on whatever things are _____, _____, .

     _____, _____, _____, of _____ _____,

     of _____, and _____.

3.   Colossians 3:1-2 – Seek those things which are _____, where Christ is, sitting at the

     right hand of God. Set your _____ on things above, not on things on the earth.

Challenge for Today

The opposite of the mind of Christ is the mind of flesh; the antidote is the truth of the word of God. Read Colossians 3:3-17. When Christ becomes our life, there are things we must put to death. From verses 5, 8 and 9 in the NKJV and the Greek definition of each term (in parentheses), I've created a list of fleshly mindsets to help us recognize those things we are to put to death now that we have the mind of Christ.

Pray, and ask the Lord which mindsets are your greatest challenge, then number the list 1 to 11, with 1 being the aspect of your greatest struggle and 11 being your least. You might not struggle with all of them all the time, but when you struggle, which ones seem to be the most common for you?

_____ Fornication (any form of sexual perversion or promiscuity, including pornography)

_____ Uncleanness (impure motives or impure, reckless, wasteful living)

_____ Passion (lust, vile or depraved passion; an affliction of the mind)

_____ Evil desire (a craving for what is wrong or destructive and doing whatever you want)

_____ Covetousness (a greedy desire for more of whatever you want, leading to idolatry)

_____ Anger (a bad temper, agitated disposition and/or violent emotion)

_____ Wrath (irritability or rash blasts of anger that quickly explode and subside)

_____ Malice (meanness or a desire to see harm come to others; disregard for laws)

_____ Blasphemy (profanity or any talk that slanders or harms another, including gossip)

_____ Filthy language (foul, low or offensive/indecent talk)

_____ Lying (deceit, including omission, or deliberately false words)

Name each of your top three fleshly mindsets below, and using the tools offered in _How to Find Something in the Bible_ in _Appendix B_, find a truth in scripture that refutes each one. For example, my number one challenge right now would be covetousness. The scripture I use to defeat this mindset is Hebrews 13:5, "Let your conduct be without covetousness; be content with such things as you have."

Mindset   Truth to Refute

1. _____   _____

                     _____

2. _____   _____

                     _____

3. _____   _____

                     _____

Now, take three index cards of any size and color. On one side, name the fleshly mindset you want to defeat with truth. On the other, write the scripture that will defeat it. Today, and for the next seven days, review your cards at least three times a day, speaking them out loud and then repeating each one as a declaration of truth for you. Using my example above, I will read the scripture as is, and then I will say: "My conduct is without covetousness. I am content with exactly what I have."

After seven days, note how God's word affected your mindsets: _____

_____

_____

_____

_____

Let's Pray: Lord, as Your children, we are so thankful to have the mind of Christ! Thank You that, as always, You provide exactly what we need to walk a walk that glorifies You. As we learn more about what that means and what that looks like, help us to recognize fleshly mindsets, and lead us to Your truth as it furthers our ability to have the mind of Christ toward others. In the sweet, holy and mighty name of Jesus, Amen.

Day 19

Do not set your mind on high things.

Scripture

Memorize today's scripture:

Do not set your mind on high things (Romans 12:16).

Stay the course with your scripture memory! Review, review, review! It will be worth every ounce of discipline you apply to commit our passage to memory. I commend you!

Teaching

Remember *phroneō* from yesterday, the Greek word for *mind*? The teacher in me can't resist a quick grammar lesson! In yesterday's life app, "Be of the same mind toward one another," *phroneō* is a noun acting as the object of the prepositional phrase, "of the same mind." The subject of yesterday's life app is assumed (You). So, "You be" is the subject/verb, and *mind* is a thing we are to share toward one another.

In today's life app, *phroneō* functions as a verb, signifying action, which in this case is selfishly seeking and striving after high things like riches, honor, exaltation and worldly power and/or influence in order to advance one's own interest or gain an advantage. When you add the adverb *not*, the message is this: "Mind *not* high things" (KJV, emphasis mine).

It's not that the high things in and of themselves are wrong, just like money isn't wrong; it's the *love* of money God says is "a root of all kinds of evil" (1 Timothy 6:10). In the same way, the problem with high things is when we *mind* them, chasing after them for the sake of what they do for us or the elevated significance we think they give us over others.

It's how we measure the worth of a thing and the worth of ourselves in light of the thing, and when the significance of the thing becomes greater than God's significance to us, it's a high thing.

What does Jesus have to say about high things? "What is highly esteemed among men is an abomination in the sight of God" (Luke 16:15). The Greek word for "what is highly esteemed" is *hypsēlos*, the same Greek word for *high things* in today's life app!

Jesus says they are an abomination, *bdelygma* in the Greek, which means "a foul thing, a detestable thing; of idols and things pertaining to idolatry."[8]

High things are idols!

Given the fact that God's first commandment to His people is, "You shall have no other gods before Me" (Exodus 20:3), it's no surprise that Satan loves to lure us with high things! Just like he did with Jesus when He was "led up by the Spirit into the wilderness to be tempted by the devil" (Matthew 4:1).

Jesus had been fasting forty days and nights. He was hungry! In this vulnerable place, Satan appealed to Jesus' pride: If you are the Son of God, prove it! First, he challenged Him to turn stones into bread, which would also have answered His gnawing stomach. Then, he dared Him to throw Himself from the pinnacle of the temple so angels could rescue Him.

Both attempts failed, and on the devil's third attempt to ensnare Jesus, we encounter our Greek word *hypsēlos*: "Again, the devil took Him up on an exceedingly high (*hypsēlos*) mountain, and showed Him all the kingdoms of the world and their glory."

All Jesus has to do to have it all in the eyes of the world is fall down and worship Satan; it's all we have to do, too. Satan might not use the same words with us today, but he employs the same tactics. He will lure us to great heights, if only we will fall down and worship him. If only we will mind high things.

But the heights to which Satan takes us lead to the depths of despair.

Jesus, too, will take us to high places; not for our destruction, but for our undivided affection. I can't wait for you to see the difference! Matthew 17:1-3 tells us, "Jesus took Peter, James, and John his brother, led them up on a high (*hypsēlos*) mountain by themselves," and there, alone with Jesus, in the high place to which He takes them, they experience His transfiguration, when "His face shone like the sun, and His clothes became as white as the light. And behold, Moses and Elijah appeared to them, talking with Him."

When Peter suggests they build three tabernacles or movable temples, one for each one, "a bright cloud overshadowed them; and suddenly a voice came out of the cloud, saying, 'This is My beloved Son, in whom I am well pleased. Hear Him!' And when the disciples heard it, they fell on their faces and were greatly afraid" (verse 5-6). When Jesus told them, "Arise, and do not be afraid," they looked up and "saw no one but Jesus only" (verses 7-8).

Do you see it? On the high mountain with Jesus, God set Him apart as the only One to worship! We must go there with Jesus. And stay there, with Jesus. And let the Lord tear down those things we want to make into idols until we see no one and nothing to worship but Jesus!

Example

In minding not high things, what are we *to* mind? The Lord always has a *do* for a *don't*, and here it is: "Seek first the kingdom of God and His righteousness, and all these things shall be added to you" (Matthew 6:33).

---

[8] "Greek Lexicon :: G946 (NKJV)." Blue Letter Bible. Sowing Circle. Web. 25 Aug, 2014.
<http://www.blueletterbible.org/lang/lexicon/lexicon.cfm?Strongs=G946&t=NKJV>.

In the Greek, *seek* is to aim and strive with an unrelenting commitment to acquire. In this case, our target is the kingdom or *basileia* of God, which refers not just to a defined domain but to the right or authority of one to rule over that domain, which in God's case is the universe and the hearts and lives of His people. As children of God saved by grace through faith in Jesus, it is His royal power, right and authority to rule and reign in every area of our lives, circumstances and relationships, as well as that of others, and it is the power given us as subjects of His rule.

So as we mind not high things, we are to relentlessly pursue not our interests, but Jesus'. Not our own power, but Jesus'. Not our own right to be in control, but Jesus'. Not the world's power and authority, but Jesus'. At the same time, we are to seek His righteousness, not in the sense of achieving good works or right behavior to somehow earn His or others' favor, but in letting the righteousness of Christ, which God credits to us when Jesus becomes our Savior, rule our thoughts, emotions and choices. In so doing, we will become increasingly honest, dependable, admirable, respectful, pure and moral in our thoughts, feelings and actions as is pleasing to God.

When we're occupied with a pursuit of what God desires, He takes care of the rest.

God will not share the space of God with anyone or anything, and He will ultimately destroy the high things we set before our eyes in such a way that we will know that He is the Lord (Ezekiel 6:1-7). And that's a great thing! Because when He does and we return to Him, He restores us and satisfies our souls to the point of wanting Him and Him alone.

Practice & Prayer

Let's look at what makes us vulnerable to idols and what to do when we find ourselves minding high things. When God met with Moses alone on Mount Sinai to instruct him on the tabernacle, priesthood, sacrifices, offerings, feasts and the law that would govern His people, Moses was gone forty days and forty nights (Exodus 24:18). In your Bible or online, look up Exodus 32:1 and fill in the blanks below:

When the people saw that Moses _____ coming down from the mountain,

the people gathered together to Aaron, and said to him, "Come, make us _____

that shall go before us; for as for this Moses, the man who brought us up out of the land

of Egypt, we do _____ _____ what has become of him.

Moses was delayed, and they became desperate for some way to satisfy their need to have something to worship. Describe a time when you sought significance, direction or comfort from someone or something other than God because you couldn't see Him, couldn't wait for Him any longer or didn't know what had become of Him.

_____

_____

_____

Have you, like Aaron, found yourself giving in to pressure to turn from God in order to have something that appears to offer more immediate satisfaction or importance? Write about it here.

_____

_____

_____

According to Ezekiel 14:6, what does God tell us to do when we have idols?

_____, turn away from your idols, and turn your faces away from all your _____.

What does 1 John 5:21 exhort us to do? _____ yourself from idols.

Challenge for Today

So there's our answer: turn away and keep away from idols. But how? Here are seven steps each of us can continually follow to guard ourselves against minding high things.

Seven Steps to Mind not High Things

1. Ask God to show you any high things in your life and be willing to hear His answer. Name them here:

   _____

   _____

   _____

2. Ask God for wisdom as to what makes you vulnerable to high things. When do you find it hard to stay your mind on Jesus and what He would have you do? Name what makes you vulnerable here:

   _____

   _____

   _____

3. Know who you are in Christ. Circle the scriptural truths that speak specifically to you today, then go back and underline the key words you need to remember always:

   God formed my inward parts; I am fearfully and wonderfully made (Psalm 139:13-14).

   God's thoughts are toward me for peace, a future and hope (Jeremiah 29:11).

   I am God's friend (John 15:15).

   I am established, anointed, sealed and guaranteed (2 Corinthians 1:21-22).

Nothing can separate me from the love of Christ (Romans 8:38-39).

God fills me with joy and peace that I may abound in hope (Romans 15:13).

I am a new creation in Christ; "all things have become new" (2 Corinthians 5:17).

I am blessed with every spiritual blessing in the heavenly places (Ephesians 1:3).

I am chosen by God to be holy and blameless before Him (Ephesians 1:4).

I am the adopted child of God according to the good pleasure of His will (Ephesians 1:5).

God will complete the good work He has begun in me (Philippians 1:6).

I have been given a spirit of power, love and a sound mind (2 Timothy 1:7).

4. Use the truth of God's word to shut down Satan's attempts to draw you into idolatry, just like Jesus did (Matthew 4:4, 7, and 10). Think about your greatest area of temptation toward idolatry. Now choose one of the above scriptures as your "weapon verse." Write it here and then memorize it.

_____

_____

_____

_____

5. Confront Satan and demand that He flee from you, just like Jesus. Look up Matthew 4:10, and write Jesus' words as your own to Satan:

_____

_____

_____

6. What is God telling you to do about your idols? Name it here: _____

What are two steps you can take toward obeying Him, starting today?

Step One: _____

Step Two: _____

7. Now obey. To know what God wants us to do is only the start. We are to "be doers of the word, and not hearers only, deceiving yourselves" (James 1:22), so give yourself a deadline for your first step:

_____

When you've done it, write down what happened and how you felt: _____

_____

_____

_____

A quick note to parents: Ezekiel 23:39 tells us parents had slain their children for their idols. Our children pay the highest price for our idolatry. We can't afford complacency. Join me, will you, in turning from idols and seeking first the kingdom of God and His righteousness? Not just because it's what God desires for us, but because it's what He desires for our children.

Let's Pray: Lord, empower us to mind not high things. Give us eyes to see Jesus, and Jesus only, as THE source of satisfaction. Guard our hearts and minds against the devil's schemes to trap us in idolatry, and please set us free! In the sweet, holy and mighty name of Jesus, Amen.

Day 20

But associate with the humble.

Scripture

Memorize today's scripture:

But associate with the humble (Romans 12:16).

Time to wrap up another verse! You know the drill: add these five words to the rest of the passages and see if you can recite the entire thing from memory. I believe in you!

Teaching

Favoritism. Popularity. The obsession to see and be seen with the "right" people, belong to the "in" crowd, post the best pics on social media or get the most likes and/or shares. Our culture is obsessed with it, even to the point of being defined by it! Celebrity sightings, name dropping...we love to be the one who knows someone or something special or holds a special position. It can be a form of the high things of yesterday's life app, to which Paul gives us the *but* today – the instead or rather:

Mind not high things; *instead*, associate with the humble.

To really get the picture of what Paul is saying, we need to look at the word *associate* in the Greek, which is *synapagō*. It is the key to understanding the true shift in perspective God requires of us as His followers.

The best way to understand *synapagō* is to picture a crowd – the energy, the force and the magnetism to see what they're seeing, do what they're doing and experience what they're experiencing. It's wanting to do what everyone else is doing so as not to stand out, be singled out or left out.

The apostle Peter did it in Antioch when he would eat with Gentiles until Jews showed up, and then "he withdrew and separated himself, fearing those who were of the circumcision" (Galatians 2:12). It was a crowd thing: "And the rest of the Jews also played the hypocrite with him, so that even Barnabas was carried away (*synapagō*) with their hypocrisy" (verse 13). Peter and Barnabas were carried away with the crowd they most wanted to impress or belong to in the moment.

If we're honest with ourselves and others, we're all susceptible to getting carried away by this force. While most of us don't live by a caste system where people are distinctly categorized and pigeonholed according to their royal or noble birthright, we do live in a culture that categorizes people by what they do and what they have.

The humble, or *tapeinos* in the Greek, are those who are literally low – socially, culturally, physically, emotionally and/or circumstantially, as well as those whose attitudes reflect their view of themselves as they truly are in light of the holiness of God: of no importance.

To associate with the humble is definitely countercultural. If you picture *synapagō* as a fast moving river, to associate with the humble is to swim upstream because the world celebrates high things, not the lowly.

It's more than going and serving these people – leaving our high places to do good deeds to people in low places, and then going right back to our comfort zones. It's to "to yield or submit one's self to lowly things, conditions, employments: not to evade their power."[9]

There's reciprocity to associating with the humble. It's sharing life, identifying with them through common experiences, not as a charitable act, but because of who we are. It's a lifestyle based on our relationship with and love for Jesus, and therefore our relationship with and love for others whom Jesus loves, regardless of their station, position or circumstances.

The *College Press NIV Commentary* explains it this way:

> Paul's point is that, insofar as we are able, we must ignore the caste distinctions and social classes imposed by our various cultures, and look upon all people, especially our Christian brothers and sisters, in the same way. The Apostle does not tell us to associate *only* with "people of low position"; he tells us rather to include these folks in our circle of friends and not to discriminate against them. It would be appropriate, though, to pay special attention to those regarded as lowly in one's particular culture, since these are the ones more likely to be shunned by the world in general.[10]

Instead of seeking to be, have or mix with the best, the celebrated and the most popular, be the one to associate with those not making a big deal of themselves and about whom no one else is making a big deal. The ones not even on the radar – the unnoticed, rejected and suffering.

I think of my friends Penny and Gary Russell. Gary felt strongly called by God to begin feeding the homeless in Houston every single Saturday morning. Penny did not, but she joined her husband anyways. At first, they fed about fifty street people from all walks of life: prostitutes, drug addicts, alcoholics, convicts, runaways, jobless. Definitely what we would call "those of humble circumstance." After associating with the homeless now since 2009, Penny and Gary and their Love Out Loud ministry (www.loveoutloudministry.org) feed 350 to 400 a week, every week. They are known as their friends. They keep their company every week. They experience what they experience, even spending two days and a night as street people in order to fully walk in their shoes.

That's the picture of today's life app. Keep company with even those in the lowest of circumstances, whether they are there by their own fault or not. Don't just pop in from our high place and do something for them. Do life with them. Do things together. These are our companions. When we think of our people, they are part of that group.

---

[9] "Greek Lexicon :: G4879 (NKJV)." Blue Letter Bible. Sowing Circle. Web. 1 Oct, 2014.
<http://www.blueletterbible.org/lang/lexicon/lexicon.cfm?Strongs=G4879&t=NKJV>.
[10] Cottrell, J. (1996). *Romans* (Vol. 2, Ro 12:16). Joplin, MO: College Press Pub. Co.

Example

The world rejects the humble; Jesus embraces them. Seeks them out. Saves them. In His eyes, lowly is not a negative. In fact, lowly is to be treasured, embraced and practiced.

Instead of seeing people and pleasure through the eyes of popularity, position and power, the Lord wants us to see people and pleasure through the eyes of Jesus, who set the ultimate example of associating with the humble.

Jesus, who came down from heaven to do His Father's will (John 6:38), and humbled Himself to the point of death. Jesus, who didn't play favorites. In fact, He sought out and spent time with the lowly and hated of society, like tax collectors, who were considered traitors and thieves. That's what Matthew was before Jesus called him to follow Him as His disciple (Matthew 9:9). By His insistence, He was a guest in the home of Zacchaeus, a chief tax collector (Luke 19:1-7).

Or the Samaritan woman at the well. Jews didn't mix with Samaritans, and to make matters worse, after having five husbands, she was living with a man who was not her husband. Yet, Jesus spent time with her (see the entire story in John 4:6-18).

Or when He washed His disciples' feet, a job reserved for the lowest rank in the room (John 13:5), teaching them:

> Do you know what I have done to you? You call Me Teacher and Lord, and you say well, for so I am. If I then, your Lord and Teacher, have washed your feet, you also ought to wash one another's feet. For I have given you an example, that you should do as I have done to you. Most assuredly, I say to you, a servant is not greater than his master; nor is he who is sent greater than he who sent him. If you know these things, blessed are you if you do them (verses 12-17).

We are blessed if we associate with the humble, for whatever we do to the least of these, we do unto Jesus. As we associate with them, and are carried away with them, we are associating and being carried away with Jesus.

Practice & Prayer

Synapagō is from the word *apagō*, which means to lead away. Where *synapagō* embodies the dynamics of a crowd or force, *apagō* is more personal – someone or something is leading another in a specific direction or to a specific destination.

Apagō is used twice in Matthew 7:13-14. Look up this passage and fill in the blanks:

> Enter by the narrow gate; for wide is the gate and broad is the way that _____
>
> to destruction, and there are many who go in by it. Because narrow is the gate and
>
> difficult is the way which _____ to life, and there are few who find it.

Jesus is leading us through the narrow gate.

For one to lead, another must follow. Who are you following, Jesus or culture? Explain here.

_____

_____

_____

What does 1 Peter 5:5b instruct us to do?

Be _____ to one another. Be clothed with _____.

What reason does Peter give for us to do so?

For "God _____ the _____, but gives _____ to the _____."

Associating with the humble isn't about doing good works. It's not about following the rules or the law, which becomes a burden. Rather, it's something we do because Jesus, by grace, is living and working in and through us.

Look up Matthew 11:29-30 and answer the following questions:

What are we to take upon ourselves? _____

How does Jesus describe His yoke? _____

How does He describe His burden? _____

Who are we to learn from? _____

How does Jesus describe Himself? _____

Everyone is equal: sinners who fall short of the glory of God (Romans 3:23). The blood of Jesus levels the playing field and erases every distinction we want to make among ourselves. To be humble is to know and understand that truth. It is the only condition in which we can receive God's grace.

Challenge for Today

Have you ever heard the saying, "living on the edge"? As we practice today's life app, let's live on the RIM: Recognize, Identify and Mix. If you're a formula lover like me, this will help you break down today's teaching into action steps that will help you carry it out in your life.

1. Recognize.

   What is a force that carries us away? Not necessarily in our emotions, but in our actions. Name what it is that you are most caught up with:

   _____

2. Identify.

Who are the "lowly" in your life? Do you know someone whose background or circumstances make them less than by the world's standards? Name them here:

_____

_____

_____

3. Mix.

Choose one of the people you named in number two. Who is it? _____

How can you *synapagō* with them? Remember, this isn't a single act of service but a way of doing life with them. You don't have to create a way. Instead, what is something you or they already are doing that you could do together?

_____

Now, make a plan. People aren't projects, but it's good to hold ourselves accountable to doing what the Lord asks us to do. Intentions aren't enough. Below, determine when, where and how are you going to carry out your intention?

By (date): _____

I will (what): _____

By (how): _____

After you've carried out your plan, be sure to come back and write what happens.

_____

_____

_____

_____

Let's Pray: Lord, Your ways are so different than ours and so incredibly superior. You bless when we do the opposite of what is natural to us. Thank You for teaching us Your ways and for working in us to will and do according to Your pleasure. May we please You in the way we associate with the humble. Open our eyes to who that is and what You would have us do in order to share life with them. In the sweet, holy and mighty name of Jesus, Amen.

Day 21

Do not be wise in your own opinion.

Scripture

Memorize today's scripture:

Do not be wise in your own opinion (Romans 12:16).

Today wraps up another verse in our passage! Commit it to memory and then review! Have you mastered the passage so far? If yes, way to go! That's your eighth verse to memorize. If not, keep on keepin' on. You'll be so glad you did.

Teaching

Ever think you know it all? Worse yet, been around someone who does? You can't get a word in edgewise, or if you do, what you say has no relevance whatsoever? There's a good chance we all do it and/or know someone who does (and they're usually no fun to be around). They are self-important, arrogant, self-reliant and prideful because they are convinced – consciously or not – that their intelligence supersedes all others, including God's.

Proverbs 26:12 tells us there is more hope for a fool than for this person. In other words, a stupid, arrogant simpleton who lacks intelligence or common sense is better off than one who is wise in his own opinion! Yikes! That's pretty strong.

We can recognize "wise-eyes syndrome" (WES) when we find ourselves discounting, dismissing or obstinately avoiding wisdom and instruction to any degree in any area of our lives. If we stubbornly and repeatedly begin our sentences with "but" followed by the reason everyone else is wrong or what they're saying doesn't apply to us, we might be suffering from WES! Viewed in that light, perhaps we can see that we all fall into this dangerous trap. In our high or low estimation of ourselves, our beliefs, attitudes, opinions, perceptions, decisions and/or direction, we drive a stake in the ground and smugly defend it. The stake then becomes a fence, and we can get trapped behind it, alone. It becomes a barrier in our relationships with God and others.

As always, God gives us the remedy! "The way of a fool is right in his own eyes, but he who heeds counsel is wise" (Proverbs 12:15).

To heed counsel is to listen, understand and obey another's advice. We must be very choosey, though, with whom we consult. And very discerning of our motives. I don't know about you, but I find it very easy to seek the counsel of those I know will agree with my opinion. It's a huge temptation for me to look for people who will confirm not challenge my thoughts and beliefs, and that's foolish too!

But even before we heed human counsel from the right counselors, we must fear the Lord: "The fear of the LORD is the beginning of wisdom, and the knowledge of the Holy One is understanding" (Proverbs 9:10).

What does it mean to "fear the Lord"? There are two aspects for us to grasp: terror and awe. On the one hand, the word *fear* may conjure up strong, negative emotions of dread and fright. In truth, that is part of it: God is a holy God and cannot tolerate sin. We should fear God, because sin always has consequences. For the unbeliever, the consequence is eternity in hell. A harsh truth, and one to be feared, until you recognize the incredible goodness and love of the heavenly Father who gives us a very simple and exact way to avoid this fate: the free gift of salvation by grace alone through faith alone in Christ alone. When we are saved, God assigns the righteousness of Jesus to us and eternally and irrevocably seals us with the Holy Spirit. When God looks at us, He sees the righteousness of Jesus, and solely on this basis, we are acceptable in His sight; we can enter into a personal relationship and intimate fellowship with our holy Father.

Yet even as believers, we must fear the Lord, because sin always has consequences, and God disciplines those He loves and punishes those He accepts as His children (Hebrews 12:6). In the same way we fear our earthly fathers when we do something wrong and know we're going to have to answer for it, we fear our heavenly Father, who won't let us get away with what is ultimately harmful to His name, to us and/or to others.

On the other hand, to "fear the Lord" is to revere, respect and admire Him. It is to wonder at His holiness, goodness, faithfulness and devotion and find ourselves in awe of Him! To fear the Lord is not an either/or but a both: be in fear and be in awe. Both demand a single response, though: worship!

Instead of being wise in our own opinion and pouring our energy into being a bigheaded fool, we should be zealous for the fear of the Lord all the day (Proverbs 23:17), seeking after it as if searching for treasure (Proverbs 2:1-5), because "the fear of the LORD leads to life, and he who has it will abide in satisfaction; He will not be visited with evil" (Proverbs 19:23).

God isn't look for know-it-alls; He's looking for those who will seek His wisdom with their all.

Example

When I think of the perfect scriptural example of being wise in one's own opinion, I think of the Pharisees – arrogant, self-proclaimed experts in the law who said one thing but did another, drawing attention to themselves and all their self-knowledge and outward obedience. Regardless of how highly they regarded themselves, here's what Jesus has to say about them in Matthew 23:

- They were hypocrites.
- They burdened others while not lifting a finger themselves.
- They did things to be noticed by men and enlarge their own borders.
- They sought places of honor and recognition.
- They were a stumbling block to others entering the kingdom of heaven.
- They followed the law outwardly but neglected justice and mercy.

- They didn't do what they ought to and did what they ought not.
- They were blind guides.
- They were fools.
- They were full of extortion and self-indulgence.
- They were like "whitewashed tombs which indeed appear beautiful outwardly, but inside are full of dead men's bones and all uncleanness" (verse 28).
- They appeared on the outside to be righteous, but inside were full of hypocrisy and lawlessness.

The conclusion of the matter? "Whoever exalts himself will be humbled, and he who humbles himself will be exalted" (verse 12).

When we are wise in our own opinion, the Lord will humble us.

Look what happens in the parable of the prodigal son found in Luke 15:11-32. Jesus tells of a brother who is wise in his own eyes and demands his inheritance of his father, who complies.

> The younger of them (the two brothers) said to his father, "Father, give me the portion of goods that falls to me." So he divided to them his livelihood. And not many days after, the younger son gathered all together, journeyed to a far country, and there wasted his possessions with prodigal living (verses 12-13, parentheses added for clarification).

While he recklessly and wastefully enjoyed his extravagant know-it-all-ness with complete abandon, a famine hit the land, and he found himself in dire straits. So "he went and joined himself to a citizen of that country, and he sent him into his fields to feed swine. And he would gladly have filled his stomach with the pods that the swine ate, and no one gave him anything" (verses 15-16).

This is where being wise in our own opinion gets us, metaphorically and many times literally.

But God. But His amazing grace.

The son recognizes his folly and repents. In his humiliation he finds humility and decides, "I will arise and go to my father, and will say to him, 'Father, I have sinned against heaven and before you, and I am no longer worthy to be called your son. Make me like one of your hired servants.' And he returned to his father" (verses 18-19).

And look at what his father does, remembering that it is representative of how our heavenly Father responds to us when He shows us our sin, we repent and we return to Him:

> And he arose and came to his father. But when he was still a great way off, his father saw him and had compassion, and ran and fell on his neck and kissed him. And the son said to him, "Father, I have sinned against heaven and in your sight, and am no longer worthy to be called your son." But the father said to his servants, "Bring out the best robe and put it on him, and put a ring on his hand and sandals on his feet. And bring the fatted calf here and kill it, and let us eat and be merry; for this my son was dead and is alive again; he was lost and is found." And they began to be merry (verses 20-24).

There is always grace and forgiveness. There is always restoration, even when there are consequences for sin. How much wiser are we to fear the Lord and avoid all the suffering of being wise in our own eyes in the first place?

Practice & Prayer

Look up Proverbs 3:5-7 in your Bible, and fill in the blanks below to discover *Seven Keys to Gaining Wisdom and Understanding*.

Seven Keys to Gaining Wisdom and Understanding

1. _____ in the _____ with all your _____.

   Our faith must rest solely in Him for our salvation and in His divine power to give to us "all things that pertain to life and godliness, through the knowledge of Him who called us by glory and virtue" (2 Peter 1:3, a familiar passage from *Day 10*).

2. _____ not on your own _____.

   We can't even trust our own thoughts toward ourselves! "But with me it is a very small thing that I should be judged by you or by a human court. In fact, I do not even judge myself. For I know of nothing against myself, yet I am not justified by this; but He who judges me is the Lord" (1 Corinthians 4:3-4).

3. In _____ your ways _____ the Lord.

   Everything we have is from Him and for His glory. As Paul explains just a few verses before our walk-the-talk passage: "For I say, through the grace given to me, to everyone who is among you, not to think of himself more highly than he ought to think, but to think soberly, as God has dealt to each one a measure of faith" (Romans 12:3). We acknowledge Him in all our ways, because all our ways come from Him.

4. He shall _____ your _____.

   "O LORD, I know the way of man is not in himself; it is not in man who walks to direct his own steps" (Jeremiah 10:23). Even when we think we know it all and are large and in charge, we're not; God is, and it is ultimately His plan that is carried out in our lives. We can plan and scheme all we want, but "a man's steps are of the LORD; how then can a man understand his own way?" (Proverbs 20:24).

5. Do not be _____ in your own _____.

   Given what we've learned so far, I think we've covered this key.

6. _____ the _____.

   See No. 5 above.

7. _____ from _____.

   "Behold, the fear of the Lord, that is wisdom, and to depart from evil is understanding" (Job 28:28). It is the natural outcome of fearing the Lord. Proverbs 16:6 tells us, "In mercy and truth Atonement is provided for iniquity; and by the fear of the LORD one departs from evil."

According to verse 8, what is the result of applying these seven keys:

It will be _____ to your _____ and _____ to your _____.

Look up Psalm 119:105 and fill in the blanks to discover the source of this wisdom and understanding:

Your _____ is a _____ to my feet and a _____ to my path.

We will find everything we need for knowledge, understanding and instruction in the word of God. Want to get wise? Get in the word, and let the word be your only opinion. Nothing else is truth, and no other thought or idea or opinion that originates in you is trustworthy. What do these two scriptures say will be the result when we do?

Proverbs 16:20   "He who _____ the word wisely will find _____ , and whoever

trusts in the LORD, _____ is he."

Proverbs 28:25-26 "He who is of a _____ heart stirs up _____ , but he who

_____ in the LORD will be _____.   He

who trusts in his _____ heart is a _____, but whoever walks

_____ will be _____."

One final thought on how to walk wisely. Find someone older and wiser than you, who loves the Lord, lives His word, is unwaveringly trustworthy and will speak God's truth in love. It's helpful, but not necessary, if they have applicable life experience that can be shared through the perspective of scriptural truth. Seek their counsel. Ask them to disciple you. If you don't have someone like this or no one comes to mind, ask the Lord to send you someone. It is His idea that we disciple one another, so He's sure to answer.

Challenge for Today

Can you think of a time when you've been wise in your own opinion? Or is there an area of your life right now where you're indulging in prideful arrogance? Look for relationships or topics where you find yourself indignant, angry and/or defensive when you're challenged. Are there thoughts, ideas and/or opinions that you're hiding because you don't want anyone to know or challenge you?

_____

_____

_____

Is there something or someone with which you're struggling and desperately don't want anyone to know? Or you're willing to talk about with people who will agree with you?

Explain here. _____

_____

_____

Are you avoiding certain people because you know they'll confront something in you? If yes, who is it and what do you not want them to address?

_____

_____

_____

When we hide our thoughts from someone who can evaluate them according to the truth of scripture, then we can be fairly sure our thoughts don't line up. Our minds can be a dangerous place to be, and when we keep others from knowing our thoughts, we can find ourselves in real peril.

Look at your responses above. Take a moment and confess these things to the Lord. Ask Him for the humility you need to be free of pride and walk in the fear of the Lord and His wisdom. Write out your prayer here.

_____

_____

_____

_____

_____

If you have an older, wiser, godly person you can talk to, set a time to meet with them to talk about what's going on in your inner life. Write your appointment time here: _____

Take today's lesson with you and share your answers with them. Trust me when I say you will be so glad you did! Confessing our sin – and pride is a sin – is freeing in the moment and freeing in the sense that it untangles us from the chains that bind us from experiencing all God has for us and the satisfaction and joy of fulfilling the purpose He has for us.

Let's Pray: Lord, open our eyes to the ways we are wise in our own opinion. Teach us what it means to fear You, and by Your Holy Spirit, empower us to walk humbly in Your ways, trusting and acknowledging You in all our ways. Thank You for the Holy Spirit, our Counselor. When we need it, please, send us godly, wise counselors who will instruct us in Your ways. In the sweet, holy and mighty name of Jesus, Amen.

Reflect & Review

Take a few minutes to look back through this week's challenges. Did you remember to write down what happened when you completed your challenges? Are there any you never got to or want to redo? Is there anything you want to make note of as a record of what you see the Lord doing or something you otherwise don't want to forget? Use this space for your thoughts.

_____

_____

_____

_____

_____

_____

_____

_____

I'd like to finish and/or repeat:

_____

_____

_____

_____

_____

_____

_____

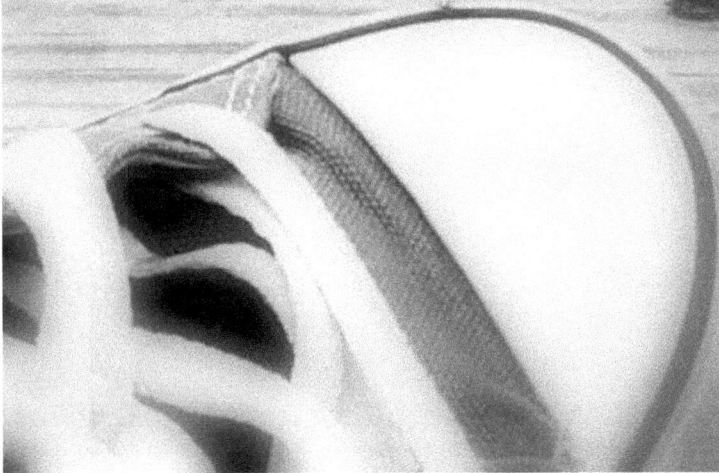

Week 5

Trusting God & letting Him be God.

Days 22-26

Lesson Five

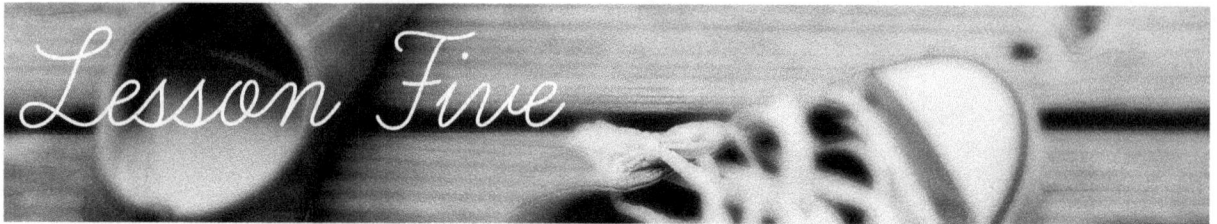

Trusting God & Letting Him Be God

Let's get into this week's lesson: _____ God and letting Him be _____!

This week's passage is Romans 12:17-19:

_____ no one evil for evil. Have regard for good things in the sight of all men. If it is possible, as much as depends on you, live peaceably with all men. Beloved, do not avenge yourselves, but rather give place to wrath; for it is written, "Vengeance is Mine, I will _____," says the Lord.

Even when a legitimate wrong _____ a just punishment, we don't get to be the one to _____ justice!

Go Ahead! Get Fat!

Instead, we need to get _____!

       F_____

       A_____

       T_____

Forgiveness Isn't Optional

When we harbor unforgiveness, we're attempting to assume a _____ and wield a _____ that belongs to God alone: being God.

God alone is sinless, righteous and holy;

we, on the other hand, when we are guilty of _____ sin,

we are guilty of them _____ (James 2:10).

We are _____ guilty as sinners regardless of the details of our sin; we all deserve the wages or what's due to us because of our sin: _____.

Applying the Right Code

Whether we admit it or not, we apply a code of _____ and _____ sin that leads to a cancerous condition called _____ by _____

We look at our sin in light of another's

and decide we're not _____ _____ as they are

so we're not _____ _____.

When God saves us, He does not give us what we deserve; instead He gives us _____ and _____. We are now righteous in God's eyes, but not by comparison; we're righteous by _____ with Jesus Christ.

Jesus' righteousness is imputed to us.

As children of God, we don't seek our _____ _____ of justice and retribution.

One Step Further: Our Debt of Love

Because we're guilty of ____ _____ and all is forgiven, we have no right to withhold forgiveness or nurse unforgiveness as _____ for retaliation. Not only that, we must take it one step further to _____ and _____ forgiveness.

"Owe no one anything except to _____ one another"

(Romans 13:8).

"For judgment is without

to the one who has shown no mercy.

Mercy _____ over judgment"

(James 2:13).

Our only _____ to others is love in mercy according to God's _____ (1 Corinthians 13:4-8).

Trusting Our Avenger

We must trust God to be our great _____; _____ is the key.

God will be _____.

Peace comes when we willingly trust Him, do what He says and let Him be _____.

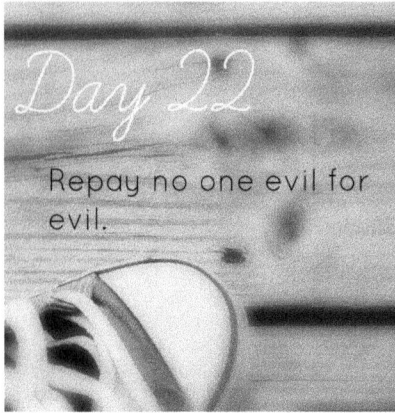

Day 22

Repay no one evil for evil.

Scripture

Memorize today's scripture:

Repay no one evil for evil (Romans 12:17).

Let's start on a new verse today. Six words. You can do it! But don't forget to review!

Teaching

This one's a whopper! I would venture to say it goes against every grain of our flesh because our sense of justice runs deep, especially when a wound is personal and painful, or when someone hurts someone we love. We want to see the right thing done. We want offenders punished. Justice served. We want life to be fair, and we want to take it upon ourselves to demand what we deem the appropriate penalty for wrong, which is exactly what Paul is telling us NOT to do.

In the Greek, *repay* conveys the idea of rendering what's due, either an appropriate punishment or payment of debt. *Evil* in the Greek has to do with things that are not as they ought to be because they are wicked and destructive.

When Paul instructs us to "repay no one evil for evil," it means that when something isn't as it should be, we don't get to make it right by doing something that isn't as it should be. When something is wicked and destructive, as children of God, we don't get to do anything wicked or destructive in reaction or response. Even when it's due.

Recently, my husband and I had an opportunity to take great offense at another person's decision. We felt betrayed, and in our opinion (yes, that's right, the opinion we don't get to be wise in), just because they had the right to do what they did didn't mean it was the right thing to do.

I'm sure if we had consulted others and spread the news about their actions, most if not all would have "taken our side." Thank God for His Spirit's restraining work in us! As we processed the shock and disappointment, we had a decision to make: would we respond in the flesh or according to the scriptures? To respond in the flesh would have been to shut this person out of our lives. Sever all ties. Hold a grudge and hang on to unforgiveness. In other words, repay evil for evil.

If, in fact, this person did us wrong, it doesn't matter. We don't get to repay the offense, justify our hurt or render judgment. The only debt we owe them is love (Romans 13:8) according to God's definition. Remember on *Day 1* when we proclaimed with our name that we love according to 1 Corinthians 13:4-8a? That's God's definition. His standard.

138

Here it is again:

> Love suffers long and is kind; love does not envy; love does not parade itself, is not puffed up; does not behave rudely, does not seek its own, is not provoked, thinks no evil; does not rejoice in iniquity, but rejoices in the truth; bears all things, believes all things, hopes all things, endures all things. Love never fails.

That pretty much rules out all forms of vengeance (we'll dig deeper into this on *Day 24* through *Day 26*)!

"But it's not right; it's wrong!" you might protest.

Yes, it is! But regardless of the evil or offense, we don't get to settle our own debts. No payback, even though it's what is due to them or it seems like the right thing to do. Instead, our energy and focus need to be directed toward doing what God desires versus what someone else deserves.

What does God desire? What is the *do* of today's *don't*? First Thessalonians 5:15 gives us the answer: "See that no one renders evil for evil to anyone, but always pursue what is good both for yourselves and for all." This is what God desires regardless of what we or others deserve. It requires us to give up the perception that it's our right to repay, and it requires forgiveness.

Example

Forgiveness is the key to freedom from the compulsion to repay evil with evil. We touched on this concept on *Day 14* as we blessed those who persecute us. We don't do it because it's easy. We do it because 1) in our sin, we have no right to judge another's sin, 2) God did it for us, and 3) God commands it. Let's take each of these one at a time.

1. In our sin, we have no right to judge another's sin.

   Remember the lady caught in adultery? (We first met her on *Day 1*, and we'll glean even more application from her story on *Day 26*.) Not one of the scribes and Pharisees, puffed up with their own pride and self-righteousness, was able to throw a stone of judgment from a place of innocence. Neither are we, whatever another's offense might be.

   We are the scribes and Pharisees when we condemn another for their sin against us. Not one man is without sin: "All have sinned and fall short of the glory of God" (Romans 3:23). And no sin is greater than another: "For whoever shall keep the whole law, and yet stumble in one point, he is guilty of all" (James 2:10). In God's economy, he who breaks one law, breaks them all. We are all equally guilty before the Lord. Let him or her who is without sin thrown the first stone.

   May I be the first to show you my empty hand?

2. God forgives us.

   When Christ died on the cross, He paid the price we owe for our sins. We deserve to be prosecuted, betrayed, persecuted, stoned, humiliated, beaten and crucified. But instead, He suffered in our place. We don't get what we deserve, and when we respond in faith to God's grace, accepting the free gift of salvation, we give up any right to exact from others the price due them for their sin.

3. We forgive as the Father has forgiven us because Jesus Himself commands it:

Jesus makes this clear in Matthew 6:14-15: "For if you forgive men their trespasses, your heavenly Father will also forgive you. But if you do not forgive men their trespasses, neither will your Father forgive your trespasses." Again, in Matthew 18:32-35, He affirms this truth through the story of an evil servant who receives forgiveness but does not extend it:

> Then his master, after he had called him, said to him, "You wicked servant! I forgave you all that debt because you begged me. Should you not also have had compassion on your fellow servant, just as I had pity on you?" And his master was angry, and delivered him to the torturers until he should pay all that was due to him. So My heavenly Father also will do to you if each of you, from his heart, does not forgive his brother his trespasses.

Unforgiveness is unacceptable. Forgiveness is a choice and act of the will. Don't wait for "feelings." Just do it, because Jesus did it for you. And every time the devil tries to remind you of the offense, proclaim your forgiveness as an act of obedience.

Drop the stone.

Practice & Prayer

What is your first reaction when you are offended? When someone hurts you in any way?

_____

_____

Think of a time when you retaliated, evil for evil? What was the result? Did it resolve things for you? Explain here.

_____

_____

Why do you think it's so hard to release justice into the hands of the Lord God Almighty? Explain here.

_____

_____

First Peter 3:8-11 gives us specific instruction in what is good for us and others. When we want to repay evil for evil, we can focus on these actions instead. Look up the passage and fill in the blanks.

(verse 8)

Be of _____ _____.

Have _____ for one another.

_____ as brothers.

Be _____.

Be _____.

(verse 9)

Return _____ with _____.

(verse 10)

Refrain your _____ from evil.

Keep your _____ from speaking deceit.

(verse 11)

Turn away from _____ and do _____.

Seek _____ and pursue it (this is our focus on Day 24).

What does verse 12 say is the result of our decision either to do good or evil?

Do good: The _____ of the LORD are on the _____, and His ears are

_____ to their _____;

Do evil: The _____ of the LORD is _____ those who do evil.

Remember on *Day 14* in *Practice & Prayer*, we looked up 1 Peter 3:15-16?

> But sanctify the Lord God in your hearts, and always be ready to give a defense to everyone who asks you a reason for the hope that is in you, with meekness and fear; having a good conscience, that when they defame you as evildoers, those who revile your good conduct in Christ may be ashamed.

What does verse 17 say?

It is _____, if it is the _____ of God, to suffer for doing _____ than

for doing _____ .

The world returns evil for evil. When we forgive and return good for evil, someone is going to want to know the reason for the hope we have – the hope that enables us to obey impossible instructions in the face of incredible evil.

If we return evil for evil, we will suffer for doing evil. Let us rather choose to suffer for doing good.

Challenge for Today

Make a list of five people and specific injuries that you need to forgive. If you need help identifying these specific individuals or offenses, ask the Lord to show you. Consider who or what you have the most intense emotional responses to when they come to mind. Fill in the first two columns of the chart below. (We'll come back to the *Good* column in a moment.)

Person	Injury or Offense	Good
_____	_____	_____
	_____	_____
_____	_____	_____
	_____	_____
_____	_____	_____
	_____	_____
_____	_____	_____
	_____	_____
_____	_____	_____
	_____	_____

Now, ask the Lord to forgive you of your unforgiveness. Confess to Him every way you have attempted to return evil for evil, even if only in the attitude of your heart and in your thoughts. As a decision of your will, decide to forgive each person and each offense. Remember, it is a choice, not a feeling.

Next, fill in the *Good* column with one specific way you can do good to each of the five people. In the next week, make it a point to do that good, for it is better to suffer for good than evil. As you do, use the space below to record what happens inside of you, with them or both!

_____

_____

_____

_____

This is a great start! We'll work more on forgiveness on *Day 24* as a means for living peaceably with all men.

Let's Pray: Lord, thank You for the power of the Holy Spirit by which we can do the impossible. Please forgive us for our unforgiveness, unbelief and all forms of judging others and seeking our own form of justice. Because You have forgiven us, we choose, as an act of obedience, to forgive others and to seek and pursue peace. In the sweet, holy and mighty name of Jesus, Amen.

Day 23

Have regard for good things in the sight of all men.

Scripture

Memorize today's scripture:

Have regard for good things in the sight of all men (Romans 12:17).

Today's verse wraps up another scripture in our passage. Commit these words to memory today, and then recite the entire passage. Continue to hide God's word in your heart!

Teaching

Today's life app is twofold: 1) having regard for good things, and 2) being watched by others. Take a look at the wording from different versions of the Bible:

"Provide things honest in the sight of all men" (KJV).

"Do things in such a way that everyone can see you are honorable" (NLT).

"Be careful to do what is right in the eyes of everyone" (NIV).

"Give thought to do what is honorable in the sight of all" (ESV).

"Try to do what is honorable in everyone's eyes" (HCSB).

"Respect what is right in the sight of all men" (NASB).

"Take thought for what is noble in the sight of all" (RSV)"

No matter what version of scripture you reference, today's life app is all about reputation – the way we live our lives before all mankind; the honest, what-you-see-is-what-you-get-and-therefore-you-can-trust-me kind of living before others.

It requires forethought, which is the essence of *have regard for*, or *proneō* in the Greek: caring enough to think ahead and consider beforehand.

Good things is from the Greek word *kalos*. The definition that captures the essence of its message is this: "excellent in its nature and characteristics, and therefore well adapted to its ends"; what's on the inside is consistent with what's seen by others, and because one is as they ought to be on the inside, what others see is "beautiful by reason of purity of heart and life, and hence praiseworthy."[11] The effect is comforting and confirming.

In 2 Corinthians 8:21, one of two other times *proneō* is used in the New Testament, Paul issues a near exact exhortation: "...providing honorable things, not only in the sight of the Lord, but also in the sight of men." He starts with *proneō* and *kalos* and ends with the same Greek words for "in the sight of men," but he adds the phrase, "not only in the sight of the Lord." In other words: Be the same in private with the Lord as you are in front of all men, because the reality is, whoever we are when only the Lord is looking is who we'll be found to be when everyone is looking.

As we learned on *Day 1*, hypocrisy hurts, because its chief end is to serve oneself by fooling others. Jesus sees right through our pretenses, and so do those who watch what we do rather than what we say.

Paul is encouraging us to care enough to think things through ahead of time so that we live genuinely in the sight of all men, especially unbelievers, that God would be glorified and Jesus exalted, and perhaps God would use us as instruments of attraction to Him.

Example

In Matthew 7:17-20, Jesus teaches:

> Even so, every good tree bears good fruit, but a bad tree bears bad fruit. A good tree cannot bear bad fruit, nor can a bad tree bear good fruit. Every tree that does not bear good fruit is cut down and thrown into the fire. Therefore, by their fruits you will know them.

What's on the inside will be known by what's seen on the outside. The only way our fruit will be good – the only way we will have regard for good things in the sight of all men – is if we are abiding in Christ in the private places of our lives. We cannot neglect our relationship with Jesus and expect to reflect Him to others. In the same way, we cannot be completely yielded to Him and behave as one who isn't His.

Jesus explains, "Abide in Me, and I in you. As the branch cannot bear fruit of itself, unless it abides in the vine, neither can you, unless you abide in Me. I am the vine, you are the branches. He who abides in Me, and I in him, bears much fruit; for without Me you can do nothing" (John 15:4-5).

The forethought of *proneō* or *having regard for* is abiding in Christ, and *kalos* or *good things* is the fruit.

When we abide in Jesus, we remain or tarry with Him, spending time in His word and in His presence. We spend time praying, worshiping and being taught and encouraged by other believers. As we do, the life that Jesus provides as the Vine produces excellence in our nature and characteristics, resulting in branches that are well adapted to their ends: bearing good fruit. And what is good fruit but a source of pleasure and nourishment for those who find it appealing?

Remember how we said the effect of *good things* is comforting and confirming? Bearing good fruit confirms because the fruit matches who we declare ourselves to be; it comforts because those who are watching can trust us to be who we say we are.

The fruit we bear will be in direct relation to the time we spend with Jesus.

---

[11] "Greek Lexicon :: G2570 (NKJV)." Blue Letter Bible. Sowing Circle. Web. 12 Dec, 2014.
<http://www.blueletterbible.org/lang/lexicon/lexicon.cfm?Strongs=G2570&t=NKJV>.

Practice & Prayer

Do you ever wish people weren't watching you? Why or why not? _____

_____

_____

Have you ever been burned because you didn't practice what you preached? Describe what happened.

_____

_____

Truth be known, it happened to me just recently. I allowed my thoughts and desires to be consumed with something I wanted of this world, and in doing so, I was abiding in my flesh, not in Christ. A resulting decision – my fruit – divulged what I longed for in the secret. When confronted with words I preached that didn't line up with what I had just done, I was humbled and heartbroken. My fruit didn't match the tree I claimed to be, and I came face-to-face with the potential harm to others, including my children and their friends, when I fail to "have regard for good things in the sight of all men."

Thank God for His forgiveness and grace! It was a humbling lesson, and I'm thankful that in love He doesn't let us get away with what He knows is harmful. Like a father, He disciplines those who are His.

Jesus continues His teaching on abiding in Him in John 15:6-10. Turn there now in your Bible, and fill in the blanks to discover *Four Steps for Abiding in Christ*.

Four Steps for Abiding in Christ

1. Know the danger of not abiding.

    If anyone does not abide in Me, he is _____ _____ as a branch and is _____;

    and they gather them throw them into the _____, and they are _____ (verse 6).

2. Know the scripture.

    If you _____ in Me, and My _____ abide in you, you will ask what

    you _____, and it shall be _____ for you (verse 7).

3. Know Jesus' love for you.

    By this My Father is _____ , that you bear much _____; so you will be

    My _____. As the Father _____ Me, I also have _____

    you; abide in My love (verses 8-9).

4. Know and do what He says to do.

If you keep My _____, you will abide in My _____, just as _____

have kept My Father's commandments and _____ in His love (verse 10).

Our fruit betrays our true affections. The more we abide in Christ, the more authentic our fruit will be.

Challenge for Today

In John 15:2, Jesus explains, "Every branch in Me that does not bear fruit He takes away; and every branch that bears fruit He prunes, that it may bear more fruit."

Let's allow the vinedresser to prune us by putting the four steps we identified above into practice below.

1. Is there an area of your life that doesn't match up in private and public? In other words, you're one thing before the Lord and another before mankind. Explain here.

_____

_____

_____

Now, take this aspect of your life to Jesus. Tell Him about it. Confess where you've neglected to abide in Him, and spend time agreeing with Him about your sin and asking for forgiveness. Abide in Jesus. Write out a prayer of confession, repentance and desired restoration here. Ask Him to make His desires your desires.

_____

_____

_____

_____

_____

Now, consider this area of your life, and think of one or two key words that would describe it. Write them here:

_____   _____

For example, if you say critical things about someone behind their back and act like a friend to that person's face, you might write down *gossip* and *hypocrisy*.

2. Now, let His word abide in you. Find a few scriptures that give you direction for what He wants you to do to line this area of your life up with His word. This is how we know His commandments. Find at least two and write them here (I've given you a few extra lines in case you find more than two):

Address _____   Scripture _____

_____   _____

_____

_____   _____

_____

_____   _____

_____

_____   _____

_____

Using our example above, you might record:

Ephesians 4:29 (NIV)   Do not let any unwholesome talk come out of your mouths, but only what is helpful for building others up according to their needs, that it may benefit those who listen.

Romans 12:9   Let love be without hypocrisy.

3. Abide in Christ, declaring His love for you and proclaiming His word over your area of struggle. Jot your prayer in response to His word here:

_____

_____

_____

_____

_____

Continuing our example above, you might say something like this:

Jesus, I know You love me, and I am Your child. I abide in Your love today. I want to bear much fruit that the Father would be glorified. As I abide in You, my talk will be wholesome and helpful for building others up according to their needs, that my words will benefit those who listen. As I abide in You, Jesus, my love will be without hypocrisy. Thank you, Father, for the genuine fruit You bring forth as I abide in the Vine today. In Jesus' name, Amen.

4. Now, do the scriptures you identified. What are two specific things you can do to line your actions up with God's word? Write them here, and then do them.

One: _____

Two: _____

Finishing our example, you might say:

One: When tempted to say something negative about someone else, I will remain silent, and if I can think of something positive, I will say that instead.

Two: To show genuine love to that person, I will go out of my way to tell them something kind.

So, if you normally complain to another person about a certain somebody in your life, speak something you appreciate about them instead, and then go to them and share that very thing with them. Love them without hypocrisy.

Abide in Christ, and in Him, your regard for good things will be seen by all, including Him.

Let's Pray: Lord, we commit ourselves to abiding in the Vine. Thank You for Your pruning and for a mighty harvest of the fruits of the Spirit in our lives, that You might be glorified in us, that we would have regard for good things in the sight of all men, and that we may be a source of confirming You and comforting others. In the sweet, holy and mighty name of Jesus, Amen.

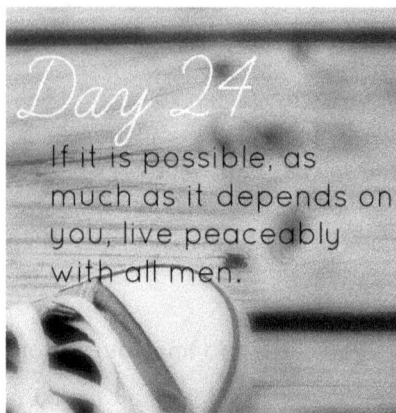

Day 24

If it is possible, as much as it depends on you, live peaceably with all men.

Scripture

Memorize today's scripture:

> *If it is possible, as much as it depends on you, live peaceably with all men (Romans 12:18).*

Today's life app is its own scripture. Let's add it to verses nine through seventeen!

Teaching

If this was football, today's life app would be an offensive play: a move to take yardage from the devil and score one for the kingdom of God! It's a proactive move to seek ways to cultivate and maintain peace, both inside yourself and with others.

Did you catch that (no pun intended!)? You must have peace within yourself first in order to have peace with others, so the application of this verse is two-fold: peace within you and peace with all men. One leads to the other, and the latter is impossible without the former.

To live peaceably, we must first know Peace. We must know Christ, be His and be reconciled to the Father in Him. Jesus Christ – the Prince of Peace – is the ultimate peacemaker. Through the cross, He reconciles us to God and to each other (Ephesians 2:12-22). This is the source for our ability to live peaceably with others.

Why is peace important? Because according to Hebrews 12:14, without it, no one will see the Lord: "Pursue peace with all people, and holiness, without which no one will see the Lord."

Notice, this scripture puts peace and holiness on equal footing. When the Prince of Peace reconciles us to God through the cross, and we are saved, we are at once at peace with God, and He produces holiness in us as He transforms and sanctifies our hearts, minds and lives. As our Father, He is faithful to complete the work He starts in us, "to will and do according to His good pleasure" (Philippians 2:13). So the peace we have with Christ becomes the source of peace with others. The outward expression of our inward holiness manifests Jesus' image, and people see Him in how we relate to others.

And yet, our life app offers two exceptions:

1. "If it is possible…" – If you have the power, might, resources, stamina, ability, influence, soul strength and can persevere under pressure or persecution; and,

2. "As much as depends on you…" – As much as all of this lies within you, is available to you and you are able to continue in it.

Why does God give us outs? Because peace isn't always possible. Our flesh will always be at war with our spirit, and sometimes our flesh will gain momentary victory. Men will reject the gospel, and in rejecting the gospel will reject us. Men will hate Jesus and hate Jesus in us. Men will pursue selfish desires and wicked schemes. The devil will be at war with God until he is cast into the lake of fire to be tormented forever (Revelation 20:10). In the meantime, God instructs us, if it is possible, as much as depends on us, live peaceably with all men.

Example

Reflect back on *Day 3* when we looked up Romans 14:19 in search of the good to which we are to cling: "Therefore let us pursue the things which make for peace and the things by which one may edify another." *Pursue* is what I would classify as a strong action verb! As we learned on *Day 14*, it means to run after swiftly with the intent of catching. Have you ever played chase or capture the flag or some other game where the goal is to go after something and capture it? That's what we're to do with peace: go after it with the goal of taking hold of it and making it ours!

If we were to play a game of *Capture the Peace*, our playbook could be built on James 3:13-18. Please take a moment to read the passage in your Bible. Here, I've used its truth to establish *Five Rules of Capture the Peace*.

Five Rules of Capture the Peace

Rule 1: Humbly submit your will to Christ.
Rule 2: Get rid of bitter envy, self-seeking and pride.
Rule 3: Seek wisdom from above.
Rule 4: Test the wisdom behind your words and actions: is it pure, peaceable, gentle, willing to yield, full of mercy and good fruits, without partiality and without hypocrisy?
Rule 5: Do what is right before the Lord.

Rules 1 through 4 require us to examine ourselves in a move toward peace on the inside, and *Rule 5* moves us toward peace with others; it will be impossible to carry out Rule 5 if we're not living out the first four. Keep in mind, this isn't an attempt to narrow Christianity down to a formula or set of rules. In using the term *rules*, it's simply an extension of the analogy that we are pursuing peace with the same intensity as we would the prize in a game of capture the flag.

So let's play!

Practice & Prayer

On *Day 14*, we learned to forgive those who hate us because they hate Jesus: the world. *Day 22* focused on forgiving specific people for legitimate wrongs they've committed against us. Today is all about humbly examining our own hearts and forgiving others for not living up to demands we knowingly or unknowingly place on them in the first place. We then must make the choice to release them from condemnation because they haven't done what we think they should and let go of the offense, anger and resentment we harbor against them as a result.

Rule 1: Humbly submit your will to Christ.

Our flesh naturally demands our own interests and perspective, even after we're saved. When we let pride have its own way, it demands of others that which it has no right to expect (to our selfish gain), and this can be our greatest barrier to peace with others. In achieving peace on the inside first, we're going to look at a non-traditional aspect of unforgiveness: identifying the pride of our flesh, yielding it to the will of God, letting go of what we assume is our right to demand and instead seeking what the Lord wants. It requires examining the expectations we put on others (and often don't communicate to them).

For example, recently the Lord revealed to me expectations I placed on someone close to me to act a certain way toward me. In my mind, I determined that if they loved me and were doing what they were supposed to be doing, they would be interested in the details of my life and would be my biggest fan! When they didn't meet my expectations, I judged them as failing me. As wrong. I was offended and held it against them. Mind you, I never told them how important it is to me to have their support and encouragement. I just rendered judgment and nursed bitterness for committing an unforgiveable offense against me. I had no peace within, and every interaction with them left me disappointed and in turmoil. I actually read into our conversations dynamics that weren't there because I had already judged them as what I thought they were. I couldn't even see reality until God revealed my sin toward them, and in confessing my sin to Him, the problem went away, because the problem was with me!

We may also find ourselves judging another because of sin in their lives or a sinful lifestyle, and once again, we nurse bitterness, anger and offense because they're not living according to our expectations. We might even be placing expectations on God.

Regardless of the circumstances, pride that says God or another person has no right to act or live a certain way is at the heart of our expectations, judgment and unforgiveness. It is pride that says we have the right to demand anything of another, even if it's right, which leads us to Rule 2.

Rule 2: Get rid of bitter envy, self-seeking and pride.

Peace is impossible with pride, and so is forgiveness. In order to get rid of bitter envy, self-seeking and pride, we have to know it's there. Like a patient seeking relief from symptoms must submit themselves to a thorough examination by the doctor, so must we lay ourselves down on the Lord's examining table and let the Holy Spirit search us and expose what's diseased. The words of the psalmist in Psalm 139:23-24 can be the cry of our hearts:

> Search me, O God, and know my heart; try me, and know my anxieties; and see if there is any wicked way in me, and lead me in the way everlasting.

Right now, let's ask the Holy Spirit to open our eyes to unforgiveness toward God or others. This is an important step, because by the nature of deception, we don't know when we're deceived. Only the Holy Spirit can give us eyes to see and understanding of truth. Hurt, bitterness and anger can blind us to our motives and the err of our thoughts, expectations, ideas of justice and desire for revenge. Let's pray:

Holy Spirit, I want to rid myself of all unforgiveness. On my own, I can't see the truth about myself. Please open my eyes to expectations I've put on others and ways I've taken offense because they didn't meet them. Show me ways I've judged them and am bitter, hurt and angry. I am willing that You would make me willing to forgive so that I can be forgiven. Thank You,

Holy Spirit, for Your work of reconciliation in my relationship with the Father and with others so that I can be a minister of reconciliation: a peacemaker. I ask these things in the power and name of Jesus Christ. Amen.

Now, let's get to work. We're going to complete the chart below one rule at a time, starting with Rule 2, which is our column called *Identify*. In the space provided, list any expectations you recognize you've put on others to be or act a certain way. Look for symptoms of offense, hurt, anger and bitterness.

Identify (Name your expectations.)	Confess (Admit and agree with God.)	Repent (Turn from your sin.)

Rule 3 and Rule 4: Seek wisdom from above. Test the wisdom behind your words and actions: is it pure, peaceable, gentle, willing to yield, full of mercy and good fruits, without partiality and without hypocrisy?

This is where we hold the word of God up to our hearts and agree with God about our sin, taking our eyes off others and focusing on ourselves as God sees us. As the Holy Spirit shows you your sin, fill in the *Confess* column. One at a time, out loud, confess every way you've put an expectation on someone else that you had no right to put on them. Confess every offense you've taken. Confess every judgment you've rendered. Confess your unforgiveness. Agree with God that it is sin.

Next, go back through your list and repent of every behavior that is YOUR responsibility before the Lord. Turn from your sin and submit to God's wisdom and His ways. This is where we make a different choice; we stop doing what we've always done and determine to do something different. In the *Repent* column, you might write:

> *Lord, I repent of (name your sin). I make the choice to come out of agreement with (name your sin) and I agree with You. I turn to You and Your way.*

Repeat it for every sin you've confessed, and declare your repentance one at a time out loud, as well.

Finally, in your heart and out loud to the Lord, as an act of your will, forgive those who have disappointed and hurt you. We can't make someone else seek forgiveness; we can only do something about ME. We can actively and intentionally forgive others, letting them go and releasing them from our obligations. One at a time, by name, release those on your list from your expectations, the judgments you've made about or against them and your anger and bitterness. Release them to your heavenly Father, and trust God to be and do what He says! You might say something like this:

> *Lord, I release (name) from (name specific expectations, hurt, offense and bitterness). As an act of my will in obedience to You, Lord, I release them from any obligation I've put on them toward me, and I trust them to You as I trust myself to You. I forgive them, Lord.*

This makes way for the Holy Spirit to convict and work in their hearts. It's giving place for wrath, as we'll learn on *Day 26*. And when you release the chains of unforgiveness, they fall from both parties. We are to do so seven times seventy-seven. In other words, repeatedly, without end, so take as much time as you need.

Challenge for Today

Now we're ready to make peace on the outside by seeking forgiveness from others!

Rule 5: Do what is right before the Lord.

Who have you hurt or offended? Make a list of the people you've hurt and specific offenses. Perhaps in recognizing your expectations and judgments, the Lord has revealed to you ways you have hurt the very people you judged. Don't do anything with the list right now. Just make it.

Name_____   My Offense_____

_____   _____

_____   _____

_____   _____

_____   _____

_____   _____

Now pray! Ask the Lord to forgive you for each and every offense He reveals to you, and then ask Him whom you need to approach to confess your offense and ask their forgiveness, too. Some of our offenses will be handled between just us and the Lord. This is where the wisdom from above is so important! We don't want to unnecessarily hurt someone else by confessing an offense of which they're totally unaware so we can feel exonerated. For example, when the Lord made me aware of the resentment I harbored toward the person I mentioned under Rule 1, they weren't even aware of it. I was judging them, and in doing so, I was shunning them, causing them harm in the good I was withholding in the relationship. But they had no idea of any of it! To confess my judgment, resentment and unforgiveness would have caused them injury, so it was an offense I dealt with between me and God. In repenting, the offense was made right in my heart, where it originated and took place. There was no longer any need for me to shun or withhold, so it was made right in the relationship, too.

So for today, let's start with those people on your list whom you've hurt, and both of you know it. Perhaps it's a spouse, child, parent or sibling with whom you've had a fight. You've said hateful things or even lashed out physically. Both of you know you've done wrong, but in pride, you haven't asked for forgiveness. This would be a person you'd want to approach. Make your list now:

Name_____   Known Offense_____

_____   _____

_____   _____

_____   _____

_____   _____

_____   _____

If you have more than one person on your list, ask the Lord which one He wants you to approach today.

Who is it? _____

Now reach out to them. I encourage you to do it face to face, or at least by phone. Avoid the temptation to hide behind text, social media or email. Part of humbling ourselves is being vulnerable and being willing to be uncomfortable. Honoring someone with personal interaction speaks volumes as to the genuineness of your heart. Here's what you might say:

The Lord has convicted me that when I _____ (name *your* *offense), I was wrong. Will you please forgive me?*

As the Holy Spirit leads you, repeat this process with as many as you have on your list. Take as long as you need, but don't put it off. As you do, "the peace of God, which surpasses all understanding, will guard your hearts and minds through Christ Jesus" (Philippians 4:7).

A few final thoughts on the words we choose when seeking forgiveness, and thank you for allowing me an extra long STEP today. Our game definitely went into overtime!

1. Avoid using the words "I'm sorry" unless what transpired was truly just an innocent mistake. For example, when you accidentally bump into someone and their drink spills, it's not the result of a conscious decision you made. It is a legitimate accident. "I'm sorry" is appropriate, and you will likely hear, "That's okay." Right?

   When an offense is intentional and forgiveness is necessary to restore the relationship, then the best words to use are, "When I _____, I was wrong. Will you forgive me?" Why? Because it forces us to be humble and confess what we've done, and it requires the other person to make a conscious decision to forgive without telling us what we did was okay. It's not okay that we wronged them, but it is possible to seek and receive forgiveness for the wrong. Do you see the difference? When someone pointed this out to me, it completely transformed the way I handle offenses and seek forgiveness.

2. Don't use the word *but* because it nullifies everything you've said before. For example, if you say, "When I lost my temper and screamed in your face, I was wrong. But you just made me so mad when you wouldn't listen to me!" Stated in this manner, you're still making it about what they did wrong and not what you did. Own your offense, and ask forgiveness with only one expectation: that you will get right with the Lord. Even if they don't say "Yes," you've done your part, and the rest is up to the Lord. Even if you think they need to reciprocate, remember, that's between them and God.

Let's Pray: Lord, thank You for making peace with us through Jesus' shed blood on the cross. Help us to live peaceably with all men. Convict us through Your Holy Spirit and make us willing to be willing to forgive and seek forgiveness. Give us wisdom from above by which we can be peacemakers. In the sweet, holy and mighty name of Jesus, Amen.

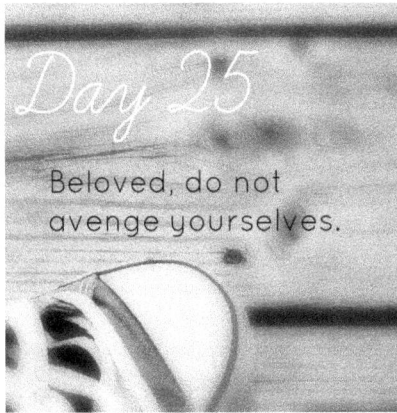

Day 25

Beloved, do not
avenge yourselves.

Scripture

Memorize today's scripture:

Beloved, do not avenge yourselves (Romans 12:19).

Keep going with your scripture memory! Can you stack today's five words on the other ten verses?

Teaching

My kids LOVE the movie *The Avengers*. There's something supremely satisfying about superheroes who use their supernatural powers to punish an evil enemy for wrongs done to those they love and the innocent. They remain on high alert and have all the tools and gadgets to detect, respond to and defeat evil! They're strong and mighty, and according to my daughter, some are extremely good looking! When the dust and smoke of the carnage of battle clears and they emerge victorious, something in us can't help but stand and cheer, as if we're the good that overcame the bad.

We want to be them, right? We want justice, which we already talked about on *Day 22*, so why today's instruction? Why does Paul tell us not to repay evil for evil in verse seventeen, and then again in verse nineteen, tell us not to avenge ourselves? What's the difference?

Maybe it's not so much of a difference as it is an extension. Someone legitimately wrongs us or someone we love, and not only are we restricted from doing something wrong in return, we don't even get to demand or exact the right consequence (unless it's our children or someone over whom we have God-given authority).

According to Proverbs 20:22, we don't even get to talk revenge: "Do not say, 'I will recompense evil.'"

How many times have we said or heard our children or someone else say: "I'm going to get you back for that!" Or we talk a big game about evening the score. Nope, we don't even get to speak it. Instead, Proverbs 20:22 goes on to say: "Wait for the LORD, and He will save you" (we'll learn more about this half of the verse tomorrow).

He will save us because He is the Avenger (1 Thessalonians 4:6). He will exact the due penalty. He will punish wrong. He is the only One who can, because He is law and justice.

So it's not about whether justice should or will be served; it's about trusting the true Avenger. Because in order to NOT take action, we have to trust that someone will, right? In order to not save ourselves or others, we have to trust that someone will.

God is the One True God. He will not share His glory with another. He tells us He is trustworthy. He proves Himself throughout history, in His word and in our lives. He tells us what He will do, and His expectation is that we will trust His trustworthiness.

If we attempt to avenge or save ourselves or others, we're doing so in unbelief. When we retaliate, it's because we don't trust God to exact justice. It's hard truth, but it's truth.

Here's some more truth about the trustworthiness of God.

TRUTH: He heeds our prayers when we put our trust in Him (1 Chronicles 5:20).

TRUTH: He defends those trust Him (Psalm 5:11).

TRUTH: If we know His name, we will trust Him and He does not forsake those who seek Him (Psalm 9:10).

TRUTH: He saves those who trust in Him (Psalm 17:7).

TRUTH: He is a shield to those who trust in Him (Psalm 18:30).

TRUTH: Trust and commit your way to the Lord and He will bring it to pass (Psalm 37:5).

TRUTH: When we fear, we can trust Him; we have nothing to fear because flesh can do nothing to us (Psalm 56:3-4). What can man do to us (verse 11)?

As Psalm 118:8 declares, "It is better to trust in the LORD than to put confidence in man," including ourselves! When we try to take things into our own hands, our unbelief is manifested in self-reliance.

No matter what happens or what He allows, we must trust Him (Job 13:15). Do not vindicate, protect or defend yourself. Trust God, without doubt, because whatever is not of faith is sin (Romans 14:23), and when we doubt God, we make ourselves unstable:

> Let him ask in faith, with no doubting, for he who doubts is like a wave of the sea driven and tossed by the wind. For let not that man suppose that he will receive anything from the Lord; he is a double-minded man, unstable in all his ways (James 1:6-8).

We either trust ourselves and believe justice is ours to serve or we trust the Lord and wait on Him. There's no both or in between. What will you choose today? Will you avenge yourself or trust the true Avenger?

(NOTE: I am in no way instructing anyone to remain in an abusive or dangerous situation or to hide crimes that should rightly be reported. If your circumstances are such, do whatever you must for your or your children's safety. It does still apply to leave the avenging of the wrong to *THE* Avenger.)

Example

In Luke 18:2-8, Jesus spoke this parable to the Pharisees:

> There was in a certain city a judge who did not fear God nor regard man. Now there was a widow in that city; and she came to him, saying, "Get justice for me from my adversary." And he would not for a while; but afterward he said within himself, "Though I do not fear God nor regard man, yet because this widow troubles me I will avenge her, lest by her continual coming she weary me." Then the Lord said, "Hear what the unjust

judge said. 'And shall God not avenge His own elect who cry out day and night to Him, though He bears long with them? I tell you that He will avenge them speedily. Nevertheless, when the Son of Man comes, will He really find faith on the earth?'"

His point is "that men always ought to pray and not lose heart" (verse 1). When we face injustice – ours or others' – our response should be to pray and trust. Yes, do what we can do to help, love, rescue, serve and encourage the victims of injustice, but we don't get to punish the unjust. (We're dealing with ourselves as individuals, here, not the role of law enforcement, government or military.)

Avenging is God's job. So we petition Him and do not lose heart in His faithfulness and power.

When Jesus returns, will the Father find faith on the earth? Will He find us standing in faith in Him? Or will He find us avenging ourselves?

Practice & Prayer

When we are victims or witnesses of injustice and we want to avenge ourselves, what do we do? Look up Psalm 25:1-5 and fill in the blanks below to find *Ten Keys to Trusting Our True Avenger*.

Ten Keys to Trusting Our True Avenger

1. _____ up your _____ – your self, life, passions and emotions, desires and will (verse 1)!

2. Choose to _____ in _____ (verse 2).

3. Do not be _____ of your God or your trust in Him (verse 2).

4. Trust God that He won't let your _____ _____ over you (verse 2).

5. Trust that when you _____ on God you will not be _____ (verse 3).

6. Know that the ones who deal treacherously without _____ will be ashamed (verse 3).

7. Ask God to _____ you His _____ and to _____ you His _____ (verse 4).

8. Ask God to _____ you in His _____ (verse 5).

9. Know _____ is the God of your _____ (verse 5).

10. _____ on God all the _____ (verse 5).

This isn't a one-time formula or something we master with finality; it's a daily process of trusting as a way of life. We might cycle through these steps once a day, once a week, once a month or all day long! We might find we're doing fine on some points, and not so great on the others. The important thing is to stay in it; never give up on God!

Challenge for Today

Name an injustice for which you'd like to be the one to deliver due punishment. What makes your blood boil when you read or hear about it? Examples might include abortion, sex trafficking or persecution.

_____

_____

What is it about this injustice that makes you want to avenge it? _____

_____

_____

Right now apply the *Ten Keys to Trusting Our True Avenger* by naming the injustice in the blanks provided below and then declaring this proclamation of trust out loud.

Lord, I lift up my soul to You – myself, my life, my passions and emotions, my desires and my

will to avenge _____ [injustice]! Instead of avenging

_____ [injustice], I trust in You, and I

will not be ashamed of You or my trust in You. I trust that You will not let my enemies

triumph in _____ [injustice]. I trust that as I wait

on You, I will not be ashamed. Rather, I trust that the ones who are dealing treacherously

without cause in _____ [injustice] will be

ashamed. Lord, show me Your ways and teach me Your paths. Lead me in Your truth. I know

You are the God of my salvation. I wait on You all the day.

Remember, "Faith comes by hearing, and hearing by the word of God" (Romans 10:17).

When we consult the word of God, we hear; when we hear from Him, we have faith. Hearing from God through His word builds our faith! To speak His word out loud delivers a double dose, which is exactly what we need when facing the urge to avenge.

Let's Pray: Lord, we do trust in You, the God of our salvation, for all things, including justice. Forgive us for every way we have convinced ourselves that we have a right to avenge ourselves. Forgive us for every form of unbelief in our hearts and every way we've relied on ourselves. Teach us Your ways and lead us in Your truth. You are the one true Avenger, and we will wait on You. In the sweet, holy and mighty name of Jesus, Amen.

Scripture

Memorize today's scripture:

But rather give place to wrath; for it is written, "Vengeance is Mine, I will repay," says the Lord (Romans 12:19).

Let's finish up verse nineteen today by adding on today's life app. We're almost to the finish line. Just two more verses after today, and you'll have the entire passage memorized. Persevere!

Teaching

Today's life app is the *do* of yesterday's *don't*: *Don't* avenge yourselves; *do* give place to wrath.

To *give place* is to wait on God. In the Greek, the message is this: grant or supply God the opportunity to punish those who do wrong. In other words, get out of the way, and let God do *His* work: vengeance. It is His and His alone, and He says He will repay. If we haven't established our trust in Him and His trustworthiness, this is going to be difficult if not impossible.

Clearly we know by now we are not His police force sent to mete out justice according to our finite understanding of people and circumstances. Again, we're approaching this from an individual not a police or military standpoint. If we attempt revenge or even entertain it in our thoughts, we are prideful as we stand in judgment over someone else, which Jesus clearly says in Matthew 7:1-5 is NOT our place:

> Judge not, that you be not judged. For with what judgment you judge, you will be judged; and with the measure you use, it will be measured back to you. And why do you look at the speck in your brother's eye, but do not consider the plank in your own eye? Or how can you say to your brother, "Let me remove the speck from your eye"; and look, a plank is in your own eye? Hypocrite! First remove the plank from your own eye, and then you will see clearly to remove the speck from your brother's eye.

It is on us to recognize and admit our own fallibility and give grace to others because we see the enormity of our own plank. And we all have one. It's called the flesh.

As we learned on *Day 21*, because of our flesh, we can't lean on our own understanding (Proverbs 3:5), not even about ourselves and what we perceive to be our own innocence or superior sense of righteousness and justice. Instead, in all our ways we are to acknowledge the Lord (verse 6) – acknowledge that He alone is God, He alone is perfect, He alone knows all, including how He'll work every circumstance to good to those who are the called according to His purpose (Romans 8:28). He alone has the right to judge, and He alone has the right to vengeance.

The problem with a plank is that it distorts our vision. Many times, when we're hurt and offended, it's not even legitimately the fault of the other person. It might be because of the unreasonable or unspoken expectations we addressed on *Day 24* or our pride or selfishness.

I know a young man who expects people to act a certain way. When they don't, he gets offended and angry. He confronts them, lectures them and demands his way, attempting to avenge what he sees as their wrong. His anger and hurt are the result of expectations he doesn't even have the right to put on other people, and many times, they don't even know he has. That's his plank not the other's speck. It's similar to the lesson the Lord took me through. By the time the Lord finished showing me my plank, I was so broken over my sin that I no longer cared about the other person's speck.

We come full circle to our *Example* on *Day 22*: when we receive undeserved grace and forgiveness from Jesus Christ, we have no right to hold anything against anyone else, whether they deserve it or not. We don't deserve God's grace. Ever. We don't deserve His forgiveness. Ever. Every single one of us *deserves* His wrath. But He extends His grace. He extends forgiveness. And when we accept it, we give up every right we think we have to judge and punish others, no matter what they've done. Because no matter what we've done, that's what God has done for us.

Example

Even Jesus, God in the form of man, gave place to the Father's wrath. He is God; He could have annihilated His enemies on the spot! But He didn't. Look at what 1 Peter 2:21-25 tells us:

> For to this you were called, because Christ also suffered for us, leaving us an example, that you should follow His steps: "Who committed no sin, nor was deceit found in His mouth"; who, when He was reviled, did not revile in return; **when He suffered, He did not threaten, but committed Himself to Him who judges righteously**; who Himself bore our sins in His own body on the tree, that we, having died to sins, might live for righteousness – by whose stripes you were healed. For you were like sheep going astray, but have now returned to the Shepherd and Overseer of your souls (emphasis mine).

Jesus is our example! When we find ourselves impatient for God's vengeance, let's remember Hebrews 12:3-4, which should put everything into perspective, even prolonged or relentless suffering:

> For consider Him who endured such hostility from sinners against Himself, lest you become weary and discouraged in your souls. You have not yet resisted to bloodshed, striving against sin.

God will not ask us to sacrifice more than Jesus already has. We simply can't, because when we put our faith in Jesus Christ, an exchange takes place. Everything He accomplished on the cross becomes ours as we become His. He *became* sin so we could be forgiven and therefore never experience the wrath of God. Because of Jesus' obedience to His Father, we will *never* suffer to the degree that Jesus did, even if we do resist to bloodshed, as many martyrs have. Therefore, we have no right to complain to God when we suffer or lose patience with His vengeance.

As Jesus gave place for wrath, so can we. The Lord will repay!

Practice & Prayer

What do we do as we give place to wrath and wait on God? Psalm 37:34 holds the key. Look it up and fill in the blanks below:

Wait on the LORD, and _____ His _____.

When we walk in His way, what does this passage say will happen?

And He shall _____ you to inherit the land; when the _____

are cut off, you shall _____ it.

Vengeance is God's; obedience is ours. As we wait, we are to do what He puts in front of us in His word. We are to do what Paul outlines for us in Romans 12:9-21. As He completes His work in us and our hearts and mindsets increasingly conform to His – as we see the planks in our own eyes – our desire will change from vengeance to humble obedience and a love for others to see them saved, not punished!

Our human nature, though, wants to rejoice when our enemies suffer, right? Look up the following scriptures and complete the warnings.

Proverbs 17:5b – He who is glad at _____ will not go _____.

Proverbs 24:17-18 – Do not _____ when your enemy _____,

and do not let your _____ be _____ when he _____;

lest the LORD see it, and it _____ Him, and He turn _____ His

wrath from him.

Our attempts at vengeance get in the way of God! We give the other person the opportunity to focus on the speck in our eyes instead of their own plank. (And we all have planks!) Instead of sitting with their own sin in a place where they have to face their honest truth before the Lord, they can instead nurse their offense at whatever we do to attempt retaliation.

Sometimes when my husband confronts me in anger about something I've done wrong, his desire to make me see and understand my wrong is thwarted by my inability to see past his delivery. I can focus on everything I see wrong about *how* he is saying it instead of facing the truth of *what* he is saying. When my kids try to get each other in trouble because they think their sister or brother deserves to be punished, many times my focus is on their wrong motive instead of what's making them so angry.

What if the scribes and Pharisees we encountered on *Day 1* and *Day 22* had stoned the woman caught in adultery? Had she lived, she could have easily nursed her hurt and anger at them, never seeing her own sin. Instead, Jesus removed the others so all she had to see was her own sin before Him. Isn't that ultimately what reconciles all relationships and circumstances, when we see our sin before Jesus and get right with Him?

When we learn to focus on our own planks, the Holy Spirit will do the work of convicting the other person. We can speak truth in love with a pure motive, but the Holy Spirit is the only One with the power to convict.

In laying down our stones and waiting on God, we leave others sitting with the truth of their own sin before Jesus and the choice to confess their sin and seek forgiveness. In this process, there is true reconciliation, with the Father and with each other. That doesn't mean all relationships will always be reconciled. Sometimes it takes both parties getting right with God about their own sin, and one party won't. Remember from *Day 24*, there are caveats to living peaceably with one another. Sometimes it's not in our power. So we do what is, and we leave the rest to God.

If there's vengeance to be had, it is the Lord's. He will repay.

Challenge for Today

Is God showing you a situation for which you need to give place to wrath and wait on Him? It can involve a person or circumstances. Explain here.

_____

_____

What is your greatest fear in giving place to God to exact His vengeance? Explain here.

_____

_____

What might happen if instead you attempt your own vengeance? _____

_____

_____

Remember, giving place to wrath doesn't mean doing nothing. It *is* an action! While we wait on Him, we are to keep His ways. What would God have you do as you give place to His wrath? What does His word tell you to do? For example, I want to make a certain person in my life see and account for the ways they're making themselves and others suffer. As I give room to God and consider what His word says I am to do instead, He is clearly instructing me to love them according to 1 Corinthians 13:4-8a *even* as they continue to ignore their plank. Write what He's telling you here.

_____

_____

_____

Now do it. Give place to God. It really is that simple, even though it's not always easy. But we must, so we can get out of His way and let His grace be the answer for us all.

Let's Pray: Lord, we confess the planks in our eyes and every way we want to focus on another's speck. We recognize that we are as deserving of Your wrath as anyone, and it is only by the blood of Jesus that we are saved. Thank You! Holy Spirit, as our Helper, help us to give place to wrath and wait on the Father to exact vengeance as He in His sovereignty determines. As we wait, teach us Your ways, that we may walk in them. Thank You, Father, in the sweet, holy and mighty name of Jesus, Amen.

Reflect & Review

Take a few minutes to look back through this week's challenges. Did you remember to write down what happened when you completed your challenges? Are there any you never got to or want to redo? Is there anything you want to make note of as a record of what you see the Lord doing or something you otherwise don't want to forget? Use this space for your thoughts.

_____

_____

_____

_____

_____

_____

_____

I'd like to finish and/or repeat:

_____

_____

_____

_____

_____

_____

Week 6

The good that overcomes evil.

Days 27-30

Lesson Six

The Good that Overcomes Evil

This week we'll study the _____ that overcomes _____, the "end of the story."

Romans 12:20-21:

> Therefore "If your enemy is hungry, feed him; if he is thirsty, give him a drink; for in so doing you will heap coals of fire on his head." Do not be _____ by evil, but overcome evil with _____.

Because Jesus is the true Avenger, good will overcome evil, _____ and_____.

Coals of Fire

As we give place to wrath and wait on God, it's not just about resisting _____; God wants us to show kindness, thereby heaping _____ coals on our enemies' heads.

We _____ our enemy with kindness,

not with a heart for revenge, but for their _____.

It goes against our human nature to respond to evil with good, yet that's exactly how God produces _____ unto salvation in us – by His _____ (Romans 2:4, ESV). By kindness, God turns His _____ into His _____. So should we!

> " Instead of allowing evil to get the upper hand and bring defeat, win the victory against that which is wrong by doing what is right…'The best way to get rid of an enemy is to turn him into a friend.' Our most powerful weapon against evil is the good. To respond to evil with evil is not to overcome it but to add to it. Believers are called upon to live victoriously in a hostile world by continuing to live as Jesus lived. Right will inevitably prevail against wrong. God is on his throne, and though all is not right in this world, he is the one who will avenge the wicked and reward the righteous." [12]

---

[12] Mounce, R. H. (1995). *Romans* (Vol. 27, pp. 241–242). Nashville: Broadman & Holman Publishers.

When an enemy of God becomes a friend of God, good replaces evil! Repentance produces _____, and the _____ in them brings about His good in them.

The Battle & Enemy

Scripture defines two very distinct _____ in the battle of good and evil:

1. _____ us.
2. _____ us.

The battle in us is between the _____ heart and spirit we receive when we're born again and the same _____ body or _____ that remains.

The battle around or outside of us is against principalities, powers, the rulers of the darkness of this age, and _____ hosts of _____ in the heavenly places.

The battle around us is spiritual warfare,

and we must "put on the whole _____ of God,

that you may be able to stand against the _____ of the devil" (Ephesians 6:11).

We cannot win in the battle between good and evil in anything but the power of God's _____ (Ephesians 6:10)! It is in the power of the Holy Spirit that we _____ protect ground that's already been taken from the devil, and_____ our position by overcoming evil with good.

Religion & Man's Rules

Let us not be among those Paul describes as "having a form of _____ while denying its _____ (2 Timothy 3:5), for it's the power that makes it _____ to walk the talk and in the end overcome evil with good! Without power, all we have is _____: man's rules and works in an attempt to earn God's _____.

Man's religion is _____ the answer; Jesus is!

Godliness with Power

The Holy Spirit is our _____. As He teaches, counsels, directs and empowers us over a lifetime, our walk will become increasingly _____ and genuinely good.

The battle against evil, inside and out, is won by our _____; striving leads to nose-diving!

In God's economy, _____is the only path to _____!

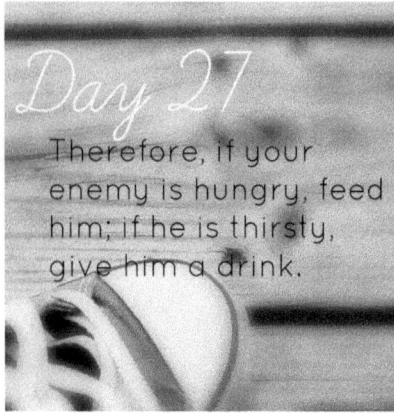

Day 27

Therefore, if your enemy is hungry, feed him; if he is thirsty, give him a drink.

Scripture

Memorize today's scripture:

> *Therefore, if your enemy is hungry, feed him; if he is thirsty, give him a drink (Romans 12:20).*

We start our second to last verse today. See if you can commit today's life app to memory and quote the entire passage so far.

Teaching

Therefore.

This is one powerful word! Think about it. What is about to be said is entirely dependent on what has already been said. If we don't know or accept the preceding content, the following content won't make sense. We won't have the information or understanding to proceed. This is entirely true of the *therefore* of today's life app, which builds on verses seventeen through nineteen.

In order to walk out today's life app, we must believe and adhere to *Day 21* through *Day 25*, all of which instruct us in how to deal with a hostile world. If we don't believe God is our Avenger and trust Him to repay, then we can't take the next step of loving and caring for our enemies. We'll be too busy with bitterness and revenge in our minds, hearts and efforts to make them pay.

Listen, if we don't believe God and trust Him, it's impossible to please Him. Hebrews 11:6 tells us, "But without faith it is impossible to please Him, for he who comes to God must believe that He is, and that He is a rewarder of those who diligently seek Him." We learned this on *Day 10*, and it's foundational to today's life app, too.

We must believe and trust God. It is the only way to truly walk the talk. When we do, the impossible He asks isn't impossible because HE makes it possible.

Like feeding our enemies, caring for them and meeting their needs.

So who is our enemy? The world would define an enemy as a rival, adversary or foe. Someone with a particular vendetta against us. They hate us specifically and act in a hostile way against us. The Bible defines an enemy as anyone who isn't a follower of Christ. They may not be hostile toward us, but their sin separates them from God, making them His enemy. This may be a hard truth to accept or understand, especially in a culture that worships tolerance and elevates it above right and wrong, but Jesus draws this line in Matthew 12:30a: "He who is not with Me is against Me."

As we saw on *Day 14*, when we follow Jesus and stand firm on His word, speaking and living His truth, the world will hate us because they hate Him. They hate Him in us. Speaking to the Pharisees, who did not believe Jesus, Jesus says in John 8:42-44:

> If God were your Father, you would love Me, for I proceeded forth and came from God; nor have I come of Myself, but He sent Me. Why do you not understand My speech? Because you are not able to listen to My word. You are of your father the devil, and the desires of your father you want to do. He was a murderer from the beginning, and does not stand in the truth, because there is no truth in him. When he speaks a lie, he speaks from his own resources, for he is a liar and the father of it.

The enemies of God suffer from not knowing Christ. They suffer in their ignorance and sin. They need the love of Jesus demonstrated through His people – us, His hands and feet. When someone is acutely aware of their need for sustenance and we, in undeserved love (like the love we receive from Christ), alleviate their suffering, it affects their hearts as it nourishes their souls! To feed them and quench their thirst is not just to give them a morsel of food or refreshing liquids. In quieting their growling stomach, we are representing the Bread of Life. In soothing a parched throat, we are smoothing the way for them to receive Living Water. The food and drink meets their physical need so they can be saturated with the truth of God's love.

Example

Before we are saved by grace through faith, we all are "alienated and enemies in your mind by wicked works" (Colossians 1:21). Yet, "God demonstrates His own love toward us, in that while we were still sinners, Christ died for us. Much more then, having now been justified by His blood, we shall be saved from wrath through Him. For if when we were enemies we were reconciled to God through the death of His Son, much more, having been reconciled, we shall be saved by His life" (Romans 5:8-10).

How much more should we, having been rescued from death and brought into life in Christ, extend the same undeserved rescue to those who hate and are hostile to us? Because really, they're not our enemies; they're His enemies. Whatever they've done to hurt and offend us is really not against us; it's because they're alienated and enemies of Christ. We can't expect someone who isn't saved to act like they are. Many times, they're doing all they know to do.

When Jesus walked the earth, He ministered to, healed, delivered, spent time with, fed and taught His enemies – enemies in that they did not know and love Him. Only in this way did His enemies become His followers. His friends. He didn't expect them to act like His friends before He saved them. He showed them how much He cared, then He saved them; then He made them His friends and instructed them in His ways. In the same way Jesus won over followers because He first loved, cared for and met their needs, so will we.

It's another opportunity for us to check our heart motive. What is our goal in following Jesus, to be blessed and enjoy the blessings, or is it to be a tool in His hands and bring glory to Him? If it's the former, then we aren't really going to be concerned about our enemy and whether or not he's hungry or thirsty. Our attitude might be, "He's chosen his lot. Let him pay the price." If it's to be a tool for Jesus' glory, then doing whatever it takes for another's salvation becomes the driving force behind loving even our enemies.

Practice & Prayer

When we see someone in need, even if it's our enemy, we are to help them. As we've learned today, we are to give them food and drink. And there's more. Look up Exodus 23:4-5 and fill in the blanks below.

If you meet your _____ ox or his donkey going _____, you shall

surely bring it back to him again. If you see the donkey of one who _____

you lying under its burden, and you would _____ from helping it, you

shall surely _____ him with it.

We may not encounter our enemy's donkey today, but the point is human nature loves to see those who harm us suffer. When someone is "getting their due," we want to stand back and rejoice. We think, "Too bad for them. They are getting what they deserve." God says to go against what feels natural to our flesh and actually go out of the way to see that our enemy does not suffer harm. Go out of our way to see that we ease their struggle. It is an act of compassion we owe to others regardless of whether they're an enemy or friend.

John MacArthur, in his commentary on Exodus 23:4-5, says:

> The attitude of impartiality was to include the helping of another with his animals regardless of whether he be friend or foe. If no help was given, his livelihood could very well be adversely affected, which was a situation others in the community could not allow to happen.[13]

Paul delivers the same message in 1 Thessalonians 5:15, which should be familiar from *Day 3* and *Day 14*. Look it up and fill in the blanks:

> See that no one renders evil for evil to anyone, but always pursue what is good both for
>
> _____ and for _____.

What is good for our enemies is good for us too. Do you see? A rising tide lifts all ships in the harbor. When we do good to our enemies, it is good for all.

Challenge for Today

Based on the definition of an enemy as anyone who is not for Christ, who would be our enemies today? Name a few here.

_____

_____

_____

---

[13] MacArthur, John. *MacArthur Study Notes (ESV)*. Bible+ by Olive Tree app.

What might it look like to see one of these enemies hungry or thirsty? If they are in our proximity, then we might encounter them in a time of need, but in some cases, we may never come face to face with one of these enemies. For example, ISIS certainly qualifies as an enemy, but we may never personally encounter them in a time of need. What would it look like to see them hungry or thirsty?

_____

_____

_____

What might it look like to feed them or give them a drink?

_____

_____

_____

Are you approaching your enemies in this way? Is the church? Write your thoughts here.

_____

_____

_____

Let's ask the Holy Spirit to give us the wisdom and strength to extend grace to our enemies, for tomorrow we will see what happens when we do.

Let's Pray: *Lord, thank You for the Holy Spirit to counsel and empower us in obeying Your word. Please show us exactly how You would have us extend grace to our enemies by feeding them and giving them drink. Use us to meet their physical needs, and in doing so, love them to You. Help us to rely on You to actually follow through in obedience. In the sweet, holy and mighty name of Jesus, Amen.*

Day 28

For in so doing, you
will heap coals of fire
on his head.

Scripture

Memorize today's scripture:

For in doing so you will heap coals of fire on his head (Romans 12:20).

Let's wrap up verse twenty today. Commit this phrase to memory and spend some time reciting the entire passage so far. You can do it!

Teaching

"For in doing so…"

These words demand that we keep yesterday's life app in the forefront of our minds as we consider today's, for in extending kindness to our enemies by meeting their physical needs, we are by default, according to God's principles, accomplishing today's!

I love the dichotomies of scripture. As only God can, He uses opposites to accomplish the supernatural. In doing exactly what we normally would never do, He accomplishes what we never could on our own.

Heap in the Greek means "to load one with the consciousness of many sins."[14] The picture of heaping coals on one's head may seem foreign or absurd to us, but in ancient Egypt, a person who wanted to publically express shame and guilt for their sins would carry a pan of burning coals on their head.

As we choose what's contrary to human nature, we're actually giving place to God to bring about the very thing that can accomplish real change: repentance. Lovingly helping someone who is against us shines light on darkness; kindness exposes hostility.

If I had to give kindness a physical description, it would be a soft, cozy blanket wrapped around my shoulders, causing me to feel warm, safe and loved. But here, God equates kindness with fire! Why?

Think about this for a moment. The intense heat of fire is unbearable. When we get too close, we either retreat or risk getting burned. Heaping burning coals on the head applies the pressure of heat to our thought life and center of understanding.

---

[14] "Greek Lexicon :: G4987 (NKJV)." Blue Letter Bible. Sowing Circle. Web. 4 Jun, 2015.
<http://www.blueletterbible.org/lang/lexicon/lexicon.cfm?Strongs=G4987&t=NKJV>.

When the Lord loads us with the painful reality of our many sins, either we retreat, because we'd rather not face the painful reality of our shortcomings, or we let the fire do its work to cleanse and refine; the heat exposes our impurities and brings them to the surface so He can skim them off.

The burning coals are the searing of the conscience and the very thing that can turn an enemy into a friend of God. Not only that, when we do things God's way, the Lord rewards us! It's the "if…then" of scripture: God says, "If you…" and then follows with a promise of what He'll do, "then I." Do the *if*, enjoy the *then*. In this case, Paul is quoting Proverbs 25:21-22, which says:

> If your enemy is hungry, give him bread to eat; and if he is thirsty, give him water to drink; for so you will heap coals of fire on his head, **and the LORD will reward you** (emphasis mine).

In Luke 6:35, Jesus says the same thing: "But love your enemies, do good, and lend, hoping for nothing in return; and your reward will be great, and you will be sons of the Most High. For He is kind to the unthankful and evil."

Jesus says our reward will be great! We don't do it for the reward, but when we do it, we can expect God's reward. What naturally follows our obedience will be "many, much, and large!"[15]

What will be our reward? The Hebrew meaning of the word holds our answer: we will have peace – with God, within ourselves and with others. God will restore us and make us whole, safe and sound as He finishes what was started.

Example

When I think of someone in the Bible who would have been clearly justified in seeking revenge, I think of David, that ruddy, good-looking shepherd boy God anoints to succeed King Saul as king of Israel. From their very first encounter, David is nothing but a yielded servant. He plays the lyre for Saul when the king is tormented by a harmful spirit. He slays the Philistine giant Goliath with a sling shot and a single stone, at which point Saul takes him and doesn't allow him to return to his father's house. Everywhere the king sends him, he is successful. Then jealousy sets in as praise for David's victories exceeds that for Saul, and from that day on, Saul determines to eliminate David. Eventually, David flees Saul and spends years on the run.

During that time, David encounters two perfect opportunities to kill Saul. First, needing to relieve himself, Saul enters a cave where David and his men are hiding. Rather than kill him, David snips a corner of the king's robe.

Another time, Saul is once again hunting David to kill him, and David finds him and his army sleeping in their camp. Rather than kill him, he steals Saul's spear and water jug from right by his head. Each time, David declines the opportunity to take his own revenge, obeying God instead, and in doing so, heaps coals of fire on Saul's head!

You can read the entire story in 1 Samuel 24 and 26, but the following is a list of nine life habits David demonstrates that lead to obedience to God and give place to His plan for redemption or wrath. In other words, here's the way to kill an enemy with kindness!

[15] "Greek Lexicon :: G4183 (NKJV)." Blue Letter Bible. Sowing Circle. Web. 29 May, 2015.
<http://www.blueletterbible.org/lang/lexicon/lexicon.cfm?Strongs=G4183&t=NKJV>.

Nine Steps to Kill an Enemy with Kindness

1. Don't listen to the voice of others. David's men see Saul's vulnerability as the Lord delivering him into David's hand, but David knows different.

2. Know what the Lord desires; obey the way of the Lord. David knows Saul is God's anointed and refuses to stretch out his hand against him.

3. Speak the truth of God's mercy to your enemy; declare their spare. Both times, David informs Saul of his mercy to spare his life, declaring his innocence.

4. Let the Lord be the judge. David refuses to judge Saul; he leaves vengeance to the Lord, for him to repay each for his behavior

5. Let the Lord convict. In sparing Saul's life, the king is confronted with his sin. He weeps, acknowledges his sin, confesses his foolishness and admits he's made a mistake.

6. Know the Lord will reward. Saul himself declares God's reward and blessing on David for his mercy to him.

7. Go the extra mile. After sparing Saul's life, even as the king continues his murderous campaign, David swears not to cut off Saul's descendants or destroy Saul's name from his father's house.

8. Go your way. Repentance doesn't always bring restoration. Even after Saul appears repentant and speaks God's reward over David for his mercy to spare his life, David maintains a distant course.

9. Know the value of your life to God and trust Him for deliverance. David captures the heart behind the how of today's life app in 1 Samuel 26:24:

   > And indeed, as your life was valued much this day in my eyes, so let my life be valued much in the eyes of the LORD, and let Him deliver me out of all tribulation.

When we know the value of our life to God and trust Him for our deliverance, we can value the eternal life of another, even our enemy. Kindness becomes our natural response and most powerful form of revenge.

Practice & Prayer

According to Romans 2:4, what does God use to lead us to repentance? _____.

Look up Ephesians 2:8 and fill in the blanks.

   For by _____ you have been saved through faith, and that not of yourselves;

   it is the _____ of God.

Now, using *www.blueletterbible.org* or another resource, look up the Greek meaning of the word *grace*, which is *charis* (Strong's G5485), and fill in the following blanks:

of the merciful _____ by which God, exerting his holy _____

upon souls, turns them to _____, keeps, strengthens, increases them in

Christian faith, knowledge, affection, and kindles them to the _____ of the

Christian virtues[16]

For every one of us, it is God's grace – His merciful kindness – that influences us to turn to Jesus Christ, at the point of salvation and every moment of every day after that! We owe this kindness to others, including our enemies, and by kindness, we are heaping coals of fire on their head! As the saying goes, "Kill 'em with kindness."

Have you ever experienced a time when someone extended kindness to you when you didn't deserve it and it was like coals of fire on your head? Describe it here.

_____

_____

_____

Has there been a time when you trusted God, extended kindness to an enemy and witnessed coals of fire bring conviction and repentance? Describe the situation here.

_____

_____

_____

Challenge for Today

We've done some serious study on enemies and forgiveness, haven't we? Starting with *Day 14* and *Day 15*, we learned to bless those who persecute us because we love Jesus. On *Day 22*, we identified specific people and offenses we need to forgive and a good we could do to each one. On *Day 24*, we examined our expectations and offenses. Moving on to *Day 25*, when we learned how to trust God when there's an injustice we want to avenge. *Day 26* focused our attention on doing what God tells us to do in His word as a way to make room for His vengeance. Then we took it a step further on *Day 27* as we were challenged to help our enemies when we see them suffering or in need.

Now today, we see God might use that very kindness to turn an enemy into a friend: His and ours. That's the "in so doing" of today's life app: showing kindness.

Refer back to your list of enemies from yesterday's *Challenge for Today* and your thoughts on what it would look like to see them in need and show them kindness.

---

[16] "Greek Lexicon :: G5485 (NKJV)." Blue Letter Bible. Sowing Circle. Web. 16 Jun, 2015.
<http://www.blueletterbible.org/lang/lexicon/lexicon.cfm?Strongs=G5485&t=NKJV>.

Based on your answers, what actions might we or the church as a whole take to encounter our enemies in their place of need? What are some specific things we could do to "heap coals of fire" on their head? Be as specific as possible in your answer.

_____

_____

_____

_____

If we did, how might it change things in the physical or in the spiritual or both?

_____

_____

_____

Identify a specific step you can take to show an enemy kindness TODAY and write a plan to take it here.

_____

_____

_____

If you're still struggling to trust God to bring conviction and repentance as you obey Him in showing kindness, take a moment to confess your resistance (okay, why don't we call it what it is: rebellion). Choose to repent and turn from your hardened heart so you can receive the heart of flesh God has for you. In fact, let's say today's prayer out loud together right now:

Let's Pray: Lord, no matter how contrary Your instruction is to our nature, we make a conscious decision right now to obey You and trust You to accomplish the work of conviction and repentance, in us and in our enemies. Thank You for Your goodness to us to lead us to repentance. We confess our rebellion against Your ways and our desire to exact our own revenge rather than yield to kindness so You can bring others to repentance. We repent, and we turn from vengeance. Thank You for using our kindness in obedience to You to turn Your enemies into friends. In the sweet, holy and mighty name of Jesus, Amen.

Now, enact your plan with no expectation of anything but God's faithfulness to your obedience. When you're done, record what happens here.

_____

_____

_____

_____

_____

Day 29

Do not be overcome by evil.

Scripture

Memorize today's scripture:

Do not be overcome by evil (Romans 12:21).

Talk about being so close to the finish line you can taste it! We are one-half of one verse from the end of having committed the entire thirteen-verse passage to memory. Let's go for it!

Teaching

The deceiver of the whole world (Revelation 12:9) is scheming against us. He wants to outwit us in order to destroy us, and we must not be ignorant of his designs (2 Corinthians 2:11). He is a thief whose only purpose and pleasure is to steal, kill and destroy (John 10:10).

Remember from *Day 21*, *evil* in the Greek has to do with things that are not as they ought to be because they are wicked and destructive. It refers to that which is wrong, detrimental, harmful, malicious and brings ruin. We are surrounded by what is evil because Satan, the god of this age, blinds the masses to the light of the gospel (2 Corinthians 4:4) – to that which brings salvation.

To not be overcome by evil will require our intentional, dedicated and constant engagement in the spiritual battle that rages around us. Lucifer started it when he rebelled against God, and he brought it to humanity when he tempted Eve to eat the apple. We are a part of it whether we want to be or not, whether we know it or not.

Evil WILL try to overcome us! We have a formidable adversary, and to not be overcome by evil is to acknowledge its existence, recognize it and resist! We must remain unmoved, anchored in Christ Jesus and His truth, because it is Jesus in us who has overcome the devil, who is in the world (1 John 4:4).

In other words, the god of this age – the god who rules everything that has to do with the world we live in, its thinking, its wisdom, its reasoning, its logic, its ways, its empty pleasures and temptations, its sin, its self-seeking destruction – can only be overcome by the Christ who lives in us.

No Christ, no victory.

Do not let evil carry off the victory! Do not let evil keep you from holding fast to your faith, even to death. Remain unmoved in the face of temptations and threats. Remain unmoved in Christ, for in dying on the cross and being raised from the dead to be seated at the right hand of God our Father – where

He is even now making intercession for those who are His – Jesus defeated the devil past, present and for eternity.

That is the Savior with whom we walk; each STEP we take is a lance in the heart of our enemy! Jesus assures us in John 16:33b, "In the world you will have tribulation; but be of good cheer, I have overcome the world." He is the One who triumphs over our adversary, and in Him, we will not be overcome by evil. As James 4:7 puts it, "Therefore submit to God. Resist the devil and he will flee from you."

Example

How do we resist the devil? In John 8:44, Jesus explains the devil "was a murderer from the beginning, and does not stand in the truth, because there is no truth in him. When he speaks a lie, he speaks from his own resources, for he is a liar and the father of it." Other versions of this same scripture say lying is consistent with his character (NLT) and when he's lying, he's speaking his native language (NIV). In other words it's all that's in him and all he knows.

If deception is the devil's means for our destruction, the truth is our greatest weapon! Let's look at the temptation of Jesus in Matthew 4:1-11, when the Spirit leads Jesus into the wilderness, where the devil attempts to trick Jesus by twisting scripture to serve his purposes. This is still his strategy today! Like Jesus, we must know what scripture says so we can recognize when it's being twisted, and we must declare truth in the face of evil, for it is the only thing that will defeat the devil.

First, Satan approaches Jesus when He is weak. He "had fasted forty days and forty nights, afterward He was hungry" (verse 2). This is when "the tempter" makes his move (verse 3), and that's when he'll make his move on us, too: when we're weak. The lesson for us is this: the devil is not all-present, all-knowing or all-powerful like our God. He is not omni anything! But he is a master of human behavior. First Peter 5:8 warns, "Be sober, be vigilant; your adversary the devil walks about like a roaring lion, seeking whom he may devour." As with Jesus it is with us: when the devil sees vulnerability, he sees an open door.

So he comes to Jesus and says, "If You are the Son of God, command that these stones become bread" (Matthew 4:3).

And Jesus answers, "**It is written**, 'Man shall not live by bread alone, but by every word that proceeds from the mouth of God'" (verse 4, emphasis mine).

Jesus is not overcome by evil; truth overcomes the devil's lie. So the devil tries again. He takes Jesus to the highest point of the temple in the holy city, and dares Him, "If You are the Son of God, throw Yourself down. For it is written: 'He shall give His angels charge over you,' and, 'In their hands they shall bear you up, lest you dash your foot against a stone'" (verse 6).

Jesus answers, "**It is written again**, 'You shall not tempt the LORD your God'" (verse 7, emphasis mine).

Notice the word, *again*. Satan does not give up easily. As Ephesians 6:13-14 stresses, we must withstand, stand and then stand some more!

So here comes the devil once more, "*Again*, the devil took Him up on an exceedingly high mountain, and showed Him all the kingdoms of the world and their glory. And he said to Him, 'All these things I will give You if You will fall down and worship me'" (Matthew 4:8-9, emphasis mine).

And Jesus stands firm, saying, "Away with you, Satan! **For it is written**, 'You shall worship the LORD your God, and Him only you shall serve'" (verse 10, emphasis mine).

Jesus didn't budge, and neither can we. It's the only way to not be overcome by evil. And when the devil finally leaves Jesus, "Behold, angels came and ministered to Him" (verse 11).

The devil will always be back. As long as the breath of life remains, he'll never finally leave us alone. He's constantly watching for another weak moment to make his move. We must be ready and remain ready. And we must believe that when we tell him to go – when in the authority given to us in Jesus' name we tell him exactly what Jesus told him, "Away with you, Satan!" – he must flee us too! And when we do, the Lord will minister to us.

Practice & Prayer

Walking the talk and resisting evil require weapons. Thank God He has armed and equipped us to overcome in Christ!

Look up Ephesians 6:11-20 and read the entire passage.

What does Paul tell us to put on in verse 11? _____

Why do we need armor?_____

Fill in the blanks for verse 12:

For we do not wrestle against _____ and _____, but

against _____, against _____, against the _____

of the _____ of this age, against _____ _____

of _____ in the _____ places.

What instruction does Paul give us *again* in verse 13? _____

Notice, this the second time Paul tells us to take up the *whole* armor of God. Don't miss this! We need *all* the armor of God, not just some. Why? What does the armor of God enable us to do?

_____

_____

According to verses 14-18, what makes up the armor of God?

Verse 14: _____ and

_____

Verse 15: _____

Verse 16: _____

182

What does Paul say we will do with the shield of faith?

_____

Verse 17: _____ and

_____

What does Paul identify as the sword of the Spirit?

_____

Verse 18: _____ and

_____

How might we put on this armor every day? _____

_____

What does Paul ask the Ephesians to pray for him in verses 19-20? Fill in the blanks.

That _____ may be given to me, that I may open my mouth _____

to make known the mystery of the _____, for which I am an ambassador

in _____; that in it I may speak _____, as I ought to speak.

Our purpose is to spread the gospel, to tell of the good news of Jesus Christ with our words and by the way we live our lives. When we secure ourselves in the armor of God each day, we will have what we need to do what He calls us to do: boldly proclaim the gospel of peace to those around us. THAT is why the devil fights against us so intensely: every salvation is a setback in his battle for souls. And every time we take up the battle against people instead of against the devil and his principalities, he gains ground.

Resist! "Give no opportunity to the devil" (Ephesians 4:27, ESV), and fight the true enemy!

Challenge for Today

Name a battle you're fighting right now – a relationship, struggle or circumstance that is threatening to overcome you. This is the "flesh and blood" the devil wants us to think is our enemy. What "skin" is the devil giving his schemes?

_____

_____

_____

For example, the "skin" of a battle the devil continually attempts to engage me in is my body image. He wants me to invest my value, time and energy into making myself beautiful and acceptable on the outside.

Remember, the only language the devil knows and speaks is lie-an-ese, so our greatest defense is truth! Grab your sword (your Bible) and find a scripture that will pierce the devil right in his lying gut! Continuing my example, the Lord clearly has shown me that hinging my happiness on my body is idolatry. So a scripture that defeats the lie of body image is Exodus 34:14, "For you shall worship no other god, for the LORD, whose name is Jealous, is a jealous God." The Lord will not share our worship!

Go ahead and write your scripture here.

_____

_____

_____

Every time the devil tries to derail you in this specific area, declare God's truth to him OUT LOUD, just like Jesus did. The devil can't read our minds. We must speak to Him as Jesus did in order to defeat him. Write out your scripture as a declaration here. You might even start with Jesus' words, "IT IS WRITTEN":

_____

_____

_____

_____

_____

This is what I declare when the devil attempts to trap me in the bondage of body image:

> *IT IS WRITTEN I shall worship no other God! My body is not my God, Jesus is, and I will worship and serve Him only!*

Let's Pray: Lord, because Christ is in us, and He who is in us is greater than he who is in the world, we will not be overcome by evil. Thank You for armor that empowers and equips us to withstand, stand and then stand! Thank You that Jesus has already overcome the devil, setting an example and accomplishing His victory in us every day. Lord God Almighty, we pray for ourselves and all the saints that we would open our mouths boldly to make known the mystery of the gospel of Jesus Christ. We are Your ambassadors, even if it be in chains. We submit to You and resist the devil. In the sweet, holy and mighty name of Jesus, Amen.

Day 30

But overcome evil
with good.

Scripture

Memorize today's scripture:

But overcome evil with good (Romans 12:21).

As they say in Hollywood, "That's a wrap!" Let's commit these last five words to memory, and then can you recite all thirteen verses? Share your victory with someone else by having them listen as you say Romans 12:9-21 out loud! And may I just say, "Congratulations!"

Teaching

Can you believe today's life app is our last one? Hang in there with me. It's another long one, but I believe you'll find it worth it!

In the spiritual battle that rages around us, we outfit ourselves daily in the armor of God and go forth onto the battle field united in one strategy: overcome evil with good. As we learned yesterday, it's not a battle we fight in the flesh with guns and armies. It's not a battle we fight with rhetoric and rancor, public service campaigns, new political leaders, social debates, legislation, strong emotional pleas or better church programs. Our good may lead to some of these things, but it is not these things in themselves that overcome evil. It's the good – the very nature of God that dwells in us, giving us a pleasant, agreeable, joyful constitution and producing in us that which is excellent, distinguished, upright and honorable[17] – that does the overcoming.

In 2 Corinthians 4:7-10, which we also referenced on *Day 14*, Paul explains:

> But we have this treasure in earthen vessels, **that the excellence of the power may be of God and not of us**. We are hard-pressed on every side, yet not crushed; we are perplexed, but not in despair; persecuted, but not forsaken; struck down, but not destroyed— always carrying about in the body the dying of the Lord Jesus, that the life of Jesus also may be manifested in our body (emphasis mine).

Today's life app is where we conquer and come off victorious, holding fast our faith against every effort of every enemy to use power, temptation or persecution to harm us. This is where we maintain the cause of Christ to the very end! It is possible because when the Spirit of God comes to dwell in us at the

---

[17] "Greek Lexicon :: G18 (NKJV)." Blue Letter Bible. Sowing Circle. Web. 30 Jun, 2015.
<http://www.blueletterbible.org/lang/lexicon/lexicon.cfm?Strongs=G18&t=NKJV>.

point of salvation, Jesus' life manifested in us *becomes* the good that overcomes evil! Remember, the good in us is the God in us: Jesus Christ!

Take a moment and really consider this. We are born dead in sin. Our hearts are wicked; our condition hopeless. Nothing good dwells in our flesh (Romans 7:18). The only way that changes is if we are born again in the Spirit (John 3:6-8). Paul explains in 1 Corinthians 12:3, "No one can say that Jesus is Lord except by the Holy Spirit."

It's grace! Remember our definition of *grace* from *Day 28*? God, by His merciful kindness, while we are yet His enemies, must exert His holy influence on our souls to turn us to Christ in faith. Even our turning to Jesus has to be God!

Once we are His, the Lord continues to exert His holy influence on us to walk according to the very Christian virtues we're learning in our *30 Days to Living a God Life not Just a Good Life: Walking in God's Ways One STEP at a Time* study. What God begins in the Spirit will be completed in the Spirit (Galatians 3:3)! Any good in us that overcomes evil is because of His initial and ongoing work in us! Our part is to yield, obey and extend the grace given us to others. It's our love and merciful kindness that will influence others for Jesus. And it's *because* of His love and merciful kindness to and in us that we extend love and merciful kindness to others.

Praise God! He has poured His love into our hearts by His Holy Spirit, and as you might remember from *Day 7*, He "is able to make all grace abound toward you, that you, always having all sufficiency in all things, may have an abundance for every good work" (2 Corinthians 9:8)!

We aren't going to overcome evil; *He* is.

Example

The key to doing good is found in 1 Peter 3:17-18, which we encountered on *Day 14* and *Day 22*:

> It is better, if it is the will of God, to suffer for doing good than for doing evil. For Christ also suffered once for sins, the just for the unjust, that He might bring us to God, being put to death in the flesh but made alive by the Spirit.

In order to overcome evil with good, we must be willing to suffer and lay down our lives *and our lifestyles* that others might be brought to God. It will be hard! It will require more of us than we have to give! But in Christ we have the perfect example, and He gives us His Spirit to accomplish it in and through us!

Let's visit the Garden of Gethsemane. Judas has just betrayed Jesus, and Jesus prays to His Father, sweating blood as He pleads, "Father, if it is Your will, take this cup away from Me; nevertheless not My will, but Yours, be done" (Luke 22:42-44).

When the chief priests and elders approach with an armed mob, His disciples attempt to respond with the sword, but Jesus commands, "Put your sword in its place, for all who take the sword will perish by the sword. Or do you think that I cannot now pray to My Father, and He will provide Me with more than twelve legions of angels?" (Matthew 26:52-53).

By my research, a Roman legion numbered anywhere from one to six thousand. So, in an instant, Jesus could have dispatched twelve to seventy-two thousand angels in His defense! If one angel in 2 Kings 19:35 killed 185,000 Assyrians, imagine what would happen with a legion of angels!

Instead, Jesus yields to His Father's will. He surrenders Himself to those who would kill Him, overcoming evil by laying down His life so that good could reign for eternity. That is the good that will overcome evil in our lives too – the laying down of our lives for God's will so that He can accomplish His eternal plan. It is how we "carry about in the body the dying of the Lord Jesus that the life of Jesus also may be manifested in our body" (2 Corinthians 4:10) as Stephen does in Acts chapters six and seven.

Stephen is described as "a man full of faith and of the Holy Spirit" (Acts 6:5), "full of grace and power" (verse 8, ESV). When those who could not "resist the wisdom and the Spirit by which he spoke" (verse 10) bring him before the council to shut him up, Stephen confronts them as "stiff-necked and uncircumcised in heart and ears" (Acts 7:51), just like the Israelites who repeatedly refused to see, believe and follow God. Even as they gnash at him and stone him, he is full of the Holy Spirit and keeps his eyes fixed on heaven. He commits his spirit to Jesus and cries out to God in a loud voice, "Lord, do not charge them with this sin" (Acts 7:54-60).

We may or may not face death for Jesus, but every one of us will be required to lay down our selves for Him in order for good to overcome evil. Here are *Six Steps to Dying to Self for Good* that we can apply from Jesus' and Stephen's examples. (Do you see the double entendre? For good as in good and good as in final!)

Six Steps to Dying to Self for Good

1. Go to the Father in prayer, even in agony, until it is His will we desire more than our own.

2. Resist temptation to fight flesh and blood with the weapons of flesh and blood.

3. Keep our eyes on Jesus, standing at the right hand of God.

4. Lay our lives in God's hands and in His care.

5. Set aside what *we* could do for what *God* would have us do, knowing that He is the ultimate guardian of our lives.

6. Remember that the goal is always the salvation of others, that the Lord would forgive their sins and reconcile them to Himself in Christ. Stephen's words echo those of Jesus' as He hangs dying on the cross: "Father, forgive them, for they do not know what they do" (Luke 23:34).

Stephen carried about in his body the dying of the Lord Jesus that the life of Jesus would be manifested in him. As it was for him, it is for us: the life of Christ in us *IS* the good that overcomes evil, and truly, with God, all things are possible (Matthew 19:26), "that the sharing of your faith may become effective by the acknowledgment of every good thing which is in you in Christ Jesus" (Philemon 1:6).

It's really very simple, but it's hard, because of what it requires of us.

Practice & Prayer

At the Last Supper with His disciples, Jesus tells them He is about to depart this earth and they will see Him no longer. Can you imagine? They are overcome with sorrow, and Jesus assures them:

> Nevertheless I tell you the truth. It is to your advantage that I go away; for if I do not go away, the Helper will not come to you; but if I depart, I will send Him to you (John 16:7).

Several names are used for *Helper* in other versions of the Bible, including Comforter, Advocate and Counselor. All of them are talking about the Holy Spirit (John 14:26). And when Jesus sends the Holy Spirit, we receive power to witness Jesus (Acts 1:8)!

In light of today's life app, why do you think the Holy Spirit is key to our walking the talk?

_____

_____

_____

Look up the following scriptures and answer the questions.

Ephesians 3:14-16 – What does the Father grant us?

_____

_____

Ephesians 3:20 – How is God able to do exceedingly abundantly above all that we ask or think?

_____

Philippians 1:19 – In addition to the prayers of his fellow believers, what does Paul recognize as the source of his deliverance?

_____

2 Peter 1:3 – How do we receive all things that pertain to life and godliness?

_____

As we established on *Day 11*, when we are saved, our bodies become temples of the Holy Spirit; He dwells in us, and we are no longer our own. Do you remember what Romans 8:1 says this means if we are in Christ Jesus? Turn there now.

_____

Not only that, Paul goes on to say, if we are in Christ Jesus, we do not _____ according to the _____, but according to the _____.

Notice the word *walk*? Since our study is on walking the talk, I find it fitting and even necessary to close by learning what Paul teaches us about walking according to the Spirit.

Read Romans 8:1-18 and Galatians 5:16-25 in their entirety, and then fill in the following blanks to discover *Twelve Truths About Walking by the Spirit*.

Twelve Truths About Walking by the Spirit

1. I must set my mind on the _____ of the _____ (Romans 8:5).

2. To set my mind on the things of the Spirit is _____ and _____ (Romans 8:6).

3. If I am in the _____ I cannot _____ God (Romans 8:8).

4. If Christ is in me, my body is _____ because of sin, but the Spirit is _____ in   me

   because of His righteousness (Romans 8:10).

5. By the _____, I will be able to put to death the deeds of the body (Romans 8:13).

6. When I walk in the Spirit, I won't fulfill the _____ of the _____ (Galatians 5:16).

7. I am _____ by the Spirit (Galatians 5:18).

8. I can _____ when I am walking in the flesh; it will be evident by the _____

   of the flesh, which are adultery, fornication, uncleanness, lewdness, idolatry, sorcery, hatred,

   contentions, jealousies, outbursts of anger, selfish ambitions, dissensions, heresies, envy,

   murder (literally, or what God equates to hatred in our hearts), drunkenness, revelries, and the

   like (Galatians 5:19-21, parentheses mine).

9. When I walk according to the _____, I will know it because I will see the _____

   of the Spirit, which is love, joy, peace, longsuffering, kindness, goodness, faithfulness,

   gentleness, and self-control (Galatians 5:22-23).

10. Because of God's Spirit in me, I do not have a spirit of _____ to fear (Romans 8:15).

11. The _____ of this present time can't be compared with my future glory (Romans 8:18).

12. If I am Christ's, I have _____ the flesh with its passions and desires; as I live in the

    _____, I will also walk in the Spirit (Galatians 5:24-25).

How does Jude 1:20-21 exhort us to maintain our walk with God? Find and list his four exhortations:

1. _____

2. _____

3. _____

4. _____

As we live the truth of 2 Timothy 3:1-7, let us not join the ranks of those he describes therein. Fill in the missing phrase:

> But know this, that in the last days perilous times will come: For men will be lovers of themselves, lovers of money, boasters, proud, blasphemers, disobedient to parents, unthankful, unholy, unloving, unforgiving, slanderers, without self-control, brutal, despisers of good, traitors, headstrong, haughty, lovers of pleasure rather than lovers of

God, _____

_____ (verse 5). And from such people turn away! For of this sort are those who creep into households and make captives of gullible women loaded down with sins, led away by various lusts, always learning and never able to come to the knowledge of the truth.

I don't know about you, but I want nothing to do with godliness as an act of my flesh, doing only what I can accomplish by my own traditions, efforts, means and control. I want godliness with power, for it's power that witnesses Jesus!

"For the kingdom of God is not in word but in power" (1 Corinthians 4:20).

The Holy Spirit dwells within us and comes upon us according to what God has for us to do; therefore all things are possible, even overcoming evil with good. Even walking the talk!

Challenge for Today

I'd like to close our study the same way we opened it, by praying Ephesians 1:15-21 for you. While I may not know you by name, I pray for you as a child of God, in faith, believing God is everything He says He is and will do everything He says He will do for you, for me and for all of His children! After receiving this prayer *over* you, please take a moment to pray it for your brethren.

Let's Pray: Thank You, Lord, for my brethren's faith in the Lord Jesus and their love for all the saints. I pray that You, Father of glory, will give Your children the spirit of wisdom and revelation in the knowledge of You. Enlighten their eyes of understanding that they may know what is the hope of Your calling, what are the riches of the glory of Your inheritance, and what is the exceeding greatness of Your power toward my brethren who believe, **according to the working of Your mighty power** which You worked in Christ when You raised Him from the dead and seated Him at Your right hand in the heavenly places, far above all principality and power and might and dominion, and every name that is named, not only in this age but also in that which is to come. Thank You, Lord, for Your Spirit, by which we as Your children are able to walk the talk You set forth in Your word. Empower my brethren afresh today! In the sweet, holy and mighty name of Jesus, Amen (emphasis mine).

Reflect & Review

Take a few minutes to look back through this week's challenges. Did you remember to write down what happened when you completed your challenges? Are there any you never got to or want to redo? Is there anything you want to make note of as a record of what you see the Lord doing or something you otherwise don't want to forget? Use this space for your thoughts.

_____

_____

_____

_____

_____

_____

_____

I'd like to finish and/or repeat:

_____

_____

_____

_____

_____

_____

Week 7

The Potter & His perfection.

Lesson Seven

Walking the Walk

This walk the Lord asks of us is _____ in our flesh, made possible only by His _____, and it leads to the _____ life Jesus promises.

In the moment when our flesh demands the _____ of what the Spirit desires, it's hard!

But in the long run, following Jesus is always the _____ choice.

The Potter & His Perfection

> "But now, O LORD, You are our Father; we are the _____, and You are our _____; and all we are the work of Your hand (Isaiah 64:8).

So we must sit on the _____ and wait for the Father to shape us into a useful _____ for His purpose and glory.

Our usefulness to Him has to be impossible for us because without faith,

it's impossible to _____ God.

Our efforts to be the potter to our own clay will only leave us feeling the _____ of our earthen vessel. But when He fills us and we become a vessel for carrying, delivering and _____ out, others will see the excellence of the _____ of God and we will experience the reality of abundant life in Christ.

When _____ of Jesus pours forth out of the private and public parts of our lives and our walk matches our talk, we represent the very One the world needs to be _____.

Perfection as God Sees It

> "Therefore you shall be perfect, just as your Father in heaven is perfect" (Matthew 5:48).

Our walk isn't about a false pursuit of perfection as the world defines it: without _____;   yet seeking the world's perfection is exactly what _____ wants because of the certain defeat it brings!

The key to God's definition of perfect is found in 2 Chronicles 16:9: "For the eyes of the LORD run to and fro throughout the whole earth, to show Himself strong on behalf of those whose _____ is _____ to Him."

Loyal = perfect = the Hebrew world *shalem* = whole, complete, at peace, safe[18]

which is from the root word *shalam* = covenant of peace[19]

When the Lord saves us, He brings us into a covenant of peace; He gives us a new _____ of flesh and puts a new _____ in us (Ezekiel 36:26). Our new heart is a _____ or loyal heart – whole, complete, at peace and safe in His hands forever.

HE won't _____ this covenant He's made with us (Psalm 89:33-34);

that's how we know we are _____ His!

The Imperfect Vessel

Our perfect heart is housed in an _____ vessel, so sometimes our actions are imperfect. Thank the Lord the perfection He's after is _____. Let us be faithful in our walk with God, and 1 Samuel 2:9 assures us, "He will guard the _____ of his faithful ones."

Being Found Faithful

Let us be found faithful! Not perfect in the sense of doing everything right on the _____ of Christian _____. Rather, perfect in that our hearts are _____ His with feet that are walking the talk on the path of life illuminated by God's _____, a path of transformation and sanctification as God completes His work in us and we learn _____.

Our next steps:

1. Continue to practice or _____ _____ the principles we've learned as the Spirit leads.

2. When we fail and sin – and we will – _____ our sin to God and others.

3. Agree with God that your sin is sin and _____ to do things His way instead.

4. Move forward in the _____, _____ and _____ of God, ready to be used by Him even in our weakness and _____.

5. _____!

[18] "H8003 - shalem (NKJV) :: Strong's Hebrew Lexicon." Blue Letter Bible. Web. 22 Mar, 2016.
<http://www.blueletterbible.org/lang/lexicon/lexicon.cfm?Strongs=H8003&t=NKJV>.
[19] "H7999 - shalam (NKJV) :: Strong's Hebrew Lexicon." Blue Letter Bible. Web. 22 Mar, 2016.
<http://www.blueletterbible.org/lang/lexicon/lexicon.cfm?Strongs=H7999&t=NKJV>.

Prayers for Faithfulness

Perhaps these prayers the Lord has put in my heart will give voice to the cry of your heart, too:

Lord, I confess that I don't love You with my whole heart, mind, strength and soul. Right now, I love [fill in the blank] more. I confess my idolatry. Lord, please forgive me and put a love in my heart for You that will change what I do!

Lord, I confess my unwillingness to obey You in [name the action or area]. Please forgive me for my [name the reason] and rebellion against You. Father, I am willing that You would make me willing to do whatever You ask whenever You ask.

Lord, I confess any unbelief. Help me to believe! Make me faithful where I am faithless, that I may please You.

I am at the end of myself, Lord. I cannot figure this out or go on in my own strength. I confess that I have been trusting in myself and not you. Lord, I repent. You are trustworthy! I trust You now.

Lord, I cannot even lean on my own understanding with regards to my own heart before You because I want to see myself so much better or worse than I am. Only You see me in truth. Please search my heart. See if there is any wicked way in me and lead me in Your way everlasting. Show me my sin and expose any way I am being deceived or believing lies. Create in me a pure heart and restore to me the joy of Your salvation.

Lord, thank You that You will not fail in Your faithfulness to us! Keep our feet on the path of faithfulness. Make our outsides match our insides so Jesus may be seen in us and glorified!

In His mighty, holy and precious name, Amen.

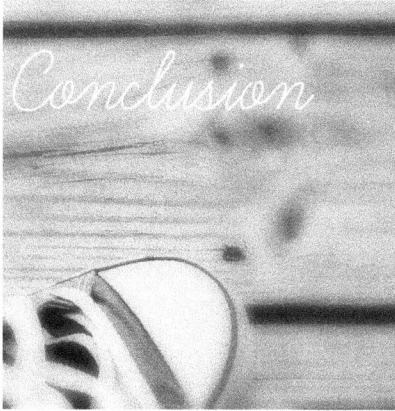

Conclusion

As I was writing *30 Days to Living a God Life not Just a Good Life: Walking in God's Ways One STEP at a Time*, I came across Psalm 86:11 and it became the cry of my heart:

> Teach me your way, O LORD,
> that I may walk in your truth;
> unite my heart to fear your name.

The longer I walk with the Lord, the more I realize the totality of His work and my utter dependence on Him to accomplish what He desires. Our walk is a yielding of our wills in the spirit, not a striving in the flesh. That's why I love this scripture! We can't walk the talk if the Lord doesn't teach us His way. His truth is the path we follow, but we won't remain there if we don't fear His name. In order to fear His name, we need Him to unite our hearts, to give us pure hearts that seek wholeheartedly after Him. We cannot love God, serve Him and walk the talk with a divided heart.

Again, I want to stress that the walk is not of works! Our study is not designed to leave us with a 30-point checklist of how to earn salvation, be the perfect Christian or secure God's favor. As Paul writes in Romans 7:6, "We have been delivered from the law, having died to what we were held by, so that we should serve in the newness of the Spirit and not in the oldness of the letter."

Remember, we don't finish in the flesh what God starts in the Spirit! Instead, Hebrews 13:20-21 affirms that it's God's work in us that produces what is pleasing to Him:

> Now may the God of peace who brought up our Lord Jesus from the dead, that great Shepherd of the sheep, through the blood of the everlasting covenant, make you complete in every good work to do His will, working in you what is well pleasing in His sight, through Jesus Christ, to whom be glory forever and ever. Amen.

We are already delivered or saved, so we're serving in obedience to bring glory to God. That means that as God teaches us His ways and unites our hearts to fear Him, we submit to Him and do as He instructs, and the walk is the evidence or outflow of the life of the Spirit of God living and working in us. It is the natural outflow as He establishes our hearts blameless in holiness (1 Thessalonians 3:13).

So what do we do now? How do we keep moving forward in our walk, learning God's truth that we may walk in it? Our answer is Romans 12:1-2:

> I beseech you therefore, brethren, by the mercies of God, that you present your bodies a living sacrifice, holy, acceptable to God, which is your reasonable service. And do not be conformed to this world, but ***be transformed by the renewing of your mind***, that you may prove what is that good and acceptable and perfect will of God (emphasis mine).

The transformation by the renewing of our minds comes by studying God's word, allowing God to teach us directly and through sound teachers, meditating on the Bible's truths, committing scripture to memory and therefore hiding it in our hearts with a result of doing what it says.

Paul pleads in 1 Thessalonians 4:1, "Finally then, brethren, we urge and exhort in the Lord Jesus that you should abound more and more, just as you received from us how you ought to walk and to please God."

There is a more and more, because God's word is infinitely alive and active. We will never reach the end of His ability to reveal and teach us more and more, to perfect us more and more, to make us more and more wholly devoted to Him.

As we walk to please God, Acts 9:31 will happen in our day too:

> Then the churches throughout all Judea, Galilee, and Samaria had peace and were edified. And walking in the fear of the Lord and in the comfort of the Holy Spirit, they were multiplied.

This is what we need now more than ever, for as God's children walk in the fear of the Lord and the comfort of the Holy Spirit, unbelievers will be saved and added to the church. Through God's saving work in a person's heart, their desires and motives can change to please Him. As that happens and the church multiplies, His good in us will overcome the evil that appears to be overtaking our world.

Together, let's walk the talk. It's life and death to those who need to see Jesus by our genuine walk.

When we walk like Jesus, we look like Jesus, giving credibility to our testimony.

Be Jesus so others can see Jesus.

Let's Pray: Lord, thank You for this time together to study the virtues of our Christian walk. By Your Holy Spirit, make each lesson a truth by which we will now live. As we live genuinely for You and before others, may our love witness Jesus. Use us to testify Him so that others may be saved, for that is our greatest good work. We love You, Lord, and are in awe of Your goodness, faithfulness and love. Thank You that You love us enough to instruct us and hold us accountable as a Daddy does His children. We long to please You, Father. In the sweet, holy and mighty name of Jesus, Amen.

Let's connect!

I would love to stay connected with you!

1. My website is www.shaunawallace.com. This is where you can find out where I'm speaking and get all kinds of updates!

   ☐ Be sure to subscribe if you want emails to come straight to your inbox!

2. Next best is social media!

   ☐ Facebook: www.facebook.com/OfficialShaunaJWallace
   ☐ Twitter: @ShaunaJWallace
   ☐ Instagram: @ShaunaJWallace
   ☐ Pinterest: www.pinterest.com/ShaunaJWallace

   (As social media changes and the next new thing is always just around the corner, please check my website for new ways to connect!)

3. Share!

   ☐ If the Lord used this study in your life, tell someone else about it.
   ☐ Suggest it to a women's Bible study group at your church or in your community.
   ☐ Tell your women's minister about it. I'll even mail her a copy with a personal note from me! Go to the *contact me* page on my website and send me her name and address, along with a little bit of background on why you'd like me to send it, the name and city of your church and any other information you think would be helpful.

4. Have me speak!

   ☐ I would love to be a part of your next women's event or retreat! Visit the *my speaking* page of my website for examples of topics and to fill out a speaker request form.

Thank you for allowing me to be a part of your journey on God's path of life!

Appendix A

The One Way of Salvation

If you feel compelled to place your faith in Jesus Christ alone for your salvation, there can only be one explanation: the Lord is giving you a new heart. Before you read any farther, will you please pray? Ask the Lord to open the eyes of your understanding and reveal to you the mystery of the gospel of Jesus Christ so that you can see the truth and the truth can set you free. For unless the Lord gives you understanding, none of this will make sense, as 1 Corinthians 12:3 and 14 explain, "No one can say that Jesus is Lord except by the Holy Spirit...the natural man does not receive the things of the Spirit of God, for they are foolishness to him; nor can he know them, because they are spiritually discerned."

Ask the Lord for spiritual discernment from His Holy Spirit, and then as you read, know that I have prayed for you, too, that you will be saved and will serve the Lord Jesus Christ every day in every way for the rest of your life.

Here's what it means to be saved, and why we're even having this conversation in the first place.

We are all born sinners; no man has any hope of *not* sinning.

Romans 3:23 tell us, "All have sinned and fall short of the glory of God."

Not one person has ever *not* sinned, except for Jesus, and not one person is capable of not sinning. From the day of our birth, we are sinners, and the Bible tells us "the wages of sin is death" (Romans 6:23a).

Even as we live and breathe physically, we are spiritually dead in our sin. Our iniquities separate us from God, and our sins have hidden His face from us (Isaiah 59:2). But it wasn't meant to be this way. When God created the heavens and the earth, He created Adam and Eve in His own image and placed them in the Garden of Eden to live in unbroken fellowship with Him. There was no sin on earth. But Satan, whose lust to be like God caused him to fall from heaven with a third of the angels, tempted Adam and Eve to eat of the one tree in the garden that God had forbidden. They did, and by this, sin entered our world. And death.

A penalty must be paid for sin; blood must be shed.

God didn't leave it there! He made a way for man to be reconciled to Him, first through a system of law and sacrifice, by which the law made God's people aware of their offenses against Him, and the blood of animals *covered* their sins. But when Jesus came to earth in the form of a man and died on the cross, He became the final sacrifice, whose blood *took away* the sin of the world. "For God so loved the world that He gave His only begotten Son, that whoever believes in Him should not perish but have everlasting life" (John 3:16).

With one man, sin entered the world and forever separated man from God. And by one Man, the penalty for sin was paid. This should cause us to rejoice!

> And not only that, but we also rejoice in God through our Lord Jesus Christ, through whom we have now received the reconciliation. Therefore, just as through one man sin entered the world, and death through sin, and thus death spread to all men, because all sinned…Therefore, as through one man's offense judgment came to all men, resulting in condemnation, even so through one Man's righteous act the free gift came to all men, resulting in justification of life. For as by one man's disobedience many were made sinners, so also by one Man's obedience many will be made righteous. Moreover the law entered that the offense might abound. But where sin abounded, grace abounded much more, so that as sin reigned in death, even so grace might reign through righteousness to eternal life through Jesus Christ our Lord (Romans 5:11-12, 18-21).

See the word *justification*? It means we're justified – made just as just-if-I'd never sinned!

Jesus died on the cross to pay the penalty for sin once and for all; He makes us just as if we'd never sinned.

When Jesus died on the cross, He took our place. He paid the price for our transgression, sin and iniquity. Psalm 32:1-2 tells us, "Blessed is he whose **transgression** is forgiven, whose **sin** is covered. Blessed is the man to whom the LORD does not impute **iniquity**, and in whose spirit there is no deceit" (emphasis mine).

Why is this important? For me, when I understand the extent of the depravity of my condition before God without Christ, it gives me a deeper appreciation of the completeness of what He did on the cross.

Iniquity is the English word for *'avon*[20], a Hebrew word for perversity, wickedness or a condition of guilt. It is the state of our heart and/or the moral corruption into which we are born because of the sin of Adam. It is the sin nature of every human that makes it impossible to *not* sin. The Bible also calls it flesh.

Encarta's definition of *perversity* perfectly captures the essence of flesh: "stubborn unreasonableness, especially willfully persisting in actions that seem contrary to good sense or your own best interests."[21] The root of *'avon* is *'avah*[22], which appropriately encompasses the idea of something being twisted, crooked, amiss or distorted, or doing perversely. This describes the state of being all of us are born into rather than a choice that we consciously make.

Transgression is the English word for *pesha'*[23], the Hebrew word that describes our rebellion and guilt as we recognize it, as God addresses it and as He forgives. It is the expression of our intrinsically corrupt condition as rebelliousness. Its root is the Hebrew word *pasha'*[24], which means to rebel, transgress or revolt. As a result of our corrupt condition from birth, we naturally revolt against God until He

---

[20] "Hebrew Lexicon :: H5771 (NKJV)." Blue Letter Bible. Sowing Circle. Web. 22 Aug, 2015. <http://www.blueletterbible.org/lang/lexicon/lexicon.cfm?Strongs=H5771&t=NKJV>.
[21] Microsoft Office Word 2007, Encarta Dictionary: English (North America).
[22] "Hebrew Lexicon :: H5753 (NKJV)." Blue Letter Bible. Sowing Circle. Web. 22 Aug, 2015. <http://www.blueletterbible.org/lang/lexicon/lexicon.cfm?Strongs=H5753&t=NKJV>.
[23] "Hebrew Lexicon :: H6588 (NKJV)." Blue Letter Bible. Sowing Circle. Web. 22 Aug, 2015. <http://www.blueletterbible.org/lang/lexicon/lexicon.cfm?Strongs=H6588&t=NKJV>.
[24] "Hebrew Lexicon :: H6586 (NKJV)." Blue Letter Bible. Sowing Circle. Web. 22 Aug, 2015. <http://www.blueletterbible.org/lang/lexicon/lexicon.cfm?Strongs=H6586&t=NKJV>.

transforms our hearts and turns us to Christ. Only then are we able to recognize our guilt, receive forgiveness and address wrong attitudes and behaviors.

The word *sin* has many roots, but in Psalm 32:1 above, the Hebrew word is *chatta'ath*[25] from the root *chata'*[26], which refers to our guilty condition because of every way we miss God's mark and stray from the path of what's right in His eyes. These are actions by which we incur guilt.

What all three of these terms tell us is this:

> We're born separated from God. Our natural state is to rebel against Him because our hearts are "deceitful above all things, and desperately wicked" (Jeremiah 17:9); when we act on that rebellion, it's sin.

No man can come to Jesus unless the Father gives him a new heart and spirit; you must be born again.

Here's the deal, and the thing that the Lord has illuminated to me in recent years. I used to think we get to choose Jesus. But Jesus clearly states in John 6:44, "No one can come to Me unless the Father who sent Me draws him; and I will raise him up at the last day."

Even before God's Son came to earth in the form of a man, conceived by the Holy Spirit and born to the virgin Mary, God promised in Ezekiel 36:26, "I will give you a new heart and put a new spirit within you; I will take the heart of stone out of your flesh and give you a heart of flesh."

Jesus explains in John 3:3 and 6-7:

> Most assuredly, I say to you, unless one is born again, he cannot see the kingdom of God... That which is born of the flesh is flesh, and that which is born of the Spirit is spirit. Do not marvel that I said to you, "You must be born again."

Without first receiving a new heart and spirit, there's no way for us to choose Jesus. A dead person with a wicked heart isn't going to choose Jesus. The Father has to first choose us!

> And you He made alive, who were dead in trespasses and sins, in which you once walked according to the course of this world, according to the prince of the power of the air, the spirit who now works in the sons of disobedience, among whom also we all once conducted ourselves in the lusts of our flesh, fulfilling the desires of the flesh and of the mind, and were by nature children of wrath, just as the others. But God, who is rich in mercy, because of His great love with which He loved us, even when we were dead in trespasses, made us alive together with Christ (by grace you have been saved), and raised us up together, and made us sit together in the heavenly places in Christ Jesus, that in the ages to come He might show the exceeding riches of His grace in His kindness toward us in Christ Jesus. For by grace you have been saved through faith, and that not of yourselves; it is the gift of God (Ephesians 2:1-8).

---

[25] "Hebrew Lexicon :: H2401 (NKJV)." Blue Letter Bible. Sowing Circle. Web. 22 Aug, 2015. <http://www.blueletterbible.org/lang/lexicon/lexicon.cfm?Strongs=H2401&t=NKJV>.
[26] "Hebrew Lexicon :: H2399 (NKJV)." Blue Letter Bible. Sowing Circle. Web. 22 Aug, 2015. <http://www.blueletterbible.org/lang/lexicon/lexicon.cfm?Strongs=H2399&t=NKJV>.

We are saved by grace alone through faith in Jesus Christ alone.

God demonstrated His love for us, "in that while we were still sinners, Christ died for us" (Romans 5:8). Remember Romans 6:23a, "For the wages of sin is death"? The rest of the verse is the rest of the story: "but the gift of God is eternal life in Christ Jesus our Lord" (Romans 6:23b).

In the Ephesians passage above, *grace* is a key word. For the longest time, grace to me referred to the good will and favor of God as demonstrated by the unearned and undeserved free gift of salvation. And it is! But when researching its Greek root *charis*[27] for my book, *Holy His: Hope for a Life and a Nation Wholly His*, another aspect of the definition forever changed my understanding of the significance of God's grace in my salvation and daily life:

> Of the merciful kindness by which God, exerting his holy influence upon souls, turns them to Christ, keeps, strengthens, increases them in Christian faith, knowledge, affection, and kindles them to the exercise of the Christian virtues.

He has to influence our soul and turn us to Christ. And when He does, we'll know He has, and we can respond in faith. There really is no other way: "Jesus said to him, 'I am the way, the truth, and the life. No one comes to the Father except through Me'" (John 14:6).

Some argue only a cruel God would allow for only one way; but I would say, it is the love of God that He makes the one way so abundantly clear! Just as there is only one way from Houston, Texas, to Dallas – traveling north – there is only one way to heaven: believe in Jesus Christ. It would not be cruel of me to direct you north to Dallas; it is the kind thing to do. To tell you to get there by any other direction would mean for you to never reach your destination!

Confess with your mouth that Jesus is Lord and believe in your heart, and you will be saved.

If you know the Lord in His merciful kindness is exerting His holy influence upon your soul and is turning you to Christ, Romans 10:9-10 instructs you on what to do now:

> If you confess with your mouth the Lord Jesus and believe in your heart that God has raised Him from the dead, you will be saved. For with the heart one believes unto righteousness, and with the mouth confession is made unto salvation.

Romans 10:13 affirms, "For 'whoever calls on the name of the LORD shall be saved.'"

There is no other way to be forgiven of our sin and eternally reconciled with God: "Nor is there salvation in any other, for there is no other name under heaven given among men by which we must be saved" (Acts 4:12).

God does the saving; we do the believing and confessing.

Are you ready to respond? "Believe on the Lord Jesus Christ, and you will be saved, you and your household" (Acts 16:31).

---

[27] "Greek Lexicon :: G5485 (NKJV)." Blue Letter Bible. Sowing Circle. Web. 28 Aug, 2015.
<http://www.blueletterbible.org/lang/lexicon/lexicon.cfm?Strongs=G5485&t=NKJV>.

Accept the gift. Respond in faith. Confess with your mouth the Lord Jesus and believe in your heart that God raised Him from the dead, and you will be saved. Your words don't save you; they are simply the evidence and confession of the new heart and spirit God has already given you by His grace and His gift of faith,

> ...having predestined us to adoption as sons by Jesus Christ to Himself, according to the good pleasure of His will, to the praise of the glory of His grace, by which He made us accepted in the Beloved. In Him we have redemption through His blood, the forgiveness of sins, according to the riches of His grace which He made to abound toward us in all wisdom and prudence, having made known to us the mystery of His will, according to His good pleasure which He purposed in Himself, that in the dispensation of the fullness of the times He might gather together in one all things in Christ, both which are in heaven and which are on earth – in Him. In Him also we have obtained an inheritance, being predestined according to the purpose of Him who works all things according to the counsel of His will (Ephesians 1:5-11).

If that is you, welcome to the family of God!

When you are His, you are His for eternity; His Spirit dwells in you!

When Jesus is our Lord, He sends the Holy Spirit as a guarantee! "Now He who establishes us with you in Christ and has anointed us is God, who also has sealed us and given us the Spirit in our hearts as a guarantee" (2 Corinthians 1:21-22).

He begins His work in us, and we can be confident that "He who has begun a good work in you will complete it until the day of Jesus Christ" (Philippians 1:6). We will not complete in our flesh – our human will, works, effort or determination – what God begins in the Spirit.

I love what Paul wrote to the Galatians, "Are you so foolish? Having begun in the Spirit, are you now being made perfect by the flesh?" (Galatians 3:3). There is nothing we can do to earn our salvation, and there's nothing we can do to keep it. In his letter to the Romans, Paul said:

> For I am persuaded that neither death nor life, nor angels nor principalities nor powers, nor things present nor things to come, 39 nor height nor depth, nor any other created thing, shall be able to separate us from the love of God which is in Christ Jesus our Lord (Romans 8:38-39).

When the Father makes us His, we are His for eternity. And He "will also confirm you to the end, that you may be blameless in the day of our Lord Jesus Christ. God is faithful, by whom you were called into the fellowship of His Son, Jesus Christ our Lord" (1 Corinthians 1:8-9). Also in 1 Thessalonians 3:12-13, we see that it is the Lord's work in us: "And may the Lord make you increase and abound in love to one another and to all, just as we do to you, so that He may establish your hearts blameless in holiness before our God and Father at the coming of our Lord Jesus Christ with all His saints."

Praise be to God that He is so faithful! But we are not off the hook. We are to be faithful to Him in obedience to His word: the Bible.

Now, follow Him!

Whatever God wants and needs to do in you, He will be faithful to do it, but there are some things He asks us to do in cooperation with Him:

> Therefore, my beloved, as you have always obeyed, not as in my presence only, but now much more in my absence, work out your own salvation with fear and trembling; for it is God who works in you both to will and to do for His good pleasure (Philippians 2:12-13).

Working out our salvation is the process by which we learn to live and love others God's way. We need to obey His truth and instructions as He has given them to us in the Bible, and we need to gather together with other believers to receive instruction and encouragement.

As Hebrews 10:24-25 establishes, we need each other in order to follow Jesus and do what the Lord asks us to do in His word:

> And let us consider one another in order to stir up love and good works, not forsaking the assembling of ourselves together, as is the manner of some, but exhorting one another, and so much the more as you see the Day approaching.

(*The Day* is the Day of Judgment when every human will stand before God Almighty, either justified by the blood of Jesus, having believed on His name for salvation and therefore having been pardoned of the penalty you rightly deserve, or condemned to eternity in hell.)

The Bible is our instruction book. It is the way we get to know our heavenly Father and what He desires of us as His ambassadors here on earth. Read it. Study it. Do what it says, knowing the same God who saved you will also, by His divine power, give to you all things for life and godliness.

Trust Him. He will show you the way, and He will equip you to follow Him.

Let's Pray: Lord, thank You that in our crooked, fallen state You don't expect us to save ourselves. Thank You for Your grace that saves us! We surrender to Your sanctifying work in our lives and to the work of the Holy Spirit as He empowers us to do what You tell us to do in Your word, not as a means for salvation, but in response to Your love and as evidence of Your salvation. In the sweet, holy and mighty name of Jesus, Amen.

Appendix B

How to Find Something in the Bible

When I want to find out what the Bible teaches about a particular topic, here are few of the tools or approaches I use. This is by no means exhaustive, and there are endless online resources and books that can instruct you on in-depth Bible study, which I encourage! What I hope to do here is simply share a few of the things I do.

The Bible

I've heard it said that BIBLE stands for Basic Instructions Before Leaving Earth. It is our manual for how to live life God's way. We must have it, read it and live by it. If you don't have a Bible, you might be overwhelmed by the number of choices available. The versions I have come to rely on are the New King James Version (NKJV), the English Standard Version (ESV), and the New American Standard Bible (NASB). Any one of these would be an excellent choice. If possible, I recommend purchasing a study Bible, which will offer notes and cross-references to help you navigate the Bible and learn more about what's going on in the scriptures and how to understand what they mean. I use *Nelson's NKJV Study Bible*.

A Concordance

I almost always start here. If I have a key word or phrase I want to research, I either use the concordance of a paper Bible or the search function of a mobile Bible app or Bible website as a launching point. Either look up the key word or phrase alphabetically in the back of your Bible or type it into the electronic resource you are using. This will produce a list of scriptures that contain that word or phrase with a brief excerpt from the verses. Don't just read the excerpt, though. Read the entire verse, and then read the scriptures before and after the use of your key word or phrase to learn the context. It's easy to misuse scripture, so this is important. If you're using an electronic Bible, most of them offer commentaries that allow you to quickly check your understanding or dig a little deeper into the context, as well.

The mobile Bible app I use is *Olive Tree: The Bible Study App*, which is free. I have purchased *The Expositor's Bible Commentary*, the *MacArthur Study Bible Notes*, the *Olive Tree Enhanced Strong's Dictionary* for referencing the Hebrew and Greek roots of words and the *Olive Tree NKJV Concordance*. All of these are available to me while I am working in my Bible study app.

The online Bible I use is *www.blueletterbible.org*, a free website that makes endless resources available at the click of your mouse. (I also use *Logos Bible Software*, but it requires a purchase). While I LOVE my mobile and online Bible resources, I grew up on a paper Bible and still have several. I use both electronic and paper versions. Because of all the study tools available at the touch of a finger or click of a mouse, I love having my Bible and study tools on my mobile device. I can add notes to scriptures, highlight verses by topic as I read through the Bible for all it teaches on a particular subject, copy and paste scriptures and passages into notes, texts, emails and on social media. Many of mobile apps have voice features that allow you to listen to the audio version, as well. I will say, though, it makes me very nervous to think of what would happen if I lost it all or if we lost power and I wasn't able to recharge my device. If possible, definitely build a paper library, but by all means, take advantage of the electronic too.

Internet Search Engines

If I don't know how to articulate a key word or phrase for what I want to research, I will sometimes ask a question of a search engine. For example, I might ask, "What guidelines does the Bible offer for dating." The word "dating" isn't in the Bible, so it would be hard to do a topic search. When I type in this question, the results lead me to a wide range of articles I can scan to find scriptures others have referenced in writing on the topic. I'm not looking for their opinions on the matter, but I do want a starting point for my own study. I'll note the scripture references I find and then go to my Bible and begin my study, looking up the scriptures and reading them in context, to the best of my ability taking into consideration all the scripture teaches on the subject.

A STRONG CAUTION: This approach introduces a bit of risk in that you will end up with results for what anyone has written, and you don't always know if they are a reliable expert that you would like to influence you in your study of the Bible. Don't take *their word* on the topic, go to *the Word*. Always.

Cross Referencing

Many times when I find a scripture on a particular topic and want to learn more, I'll see what scriptures are cross-referenced in the margin and/or study notes of my paper Bible or in the extra *guide* feature of my mobile Bible app. I'll look up those scriptures, and then I'll see what the cross-references are for those and so on until I've exhausted all leads.

Hebrew or Greek Word Study and Cross Reference

This is a favorite tool for gaining understanding about a scripture. When I want to dig deep into the meaning of a verse, I'll go to *www.blueletterbible.org* and use the *Interlinear* feature. This tool allows me to see the Hebrew (Old Testament) or Greek (New Testament) meaning of the original language of scripture. Once I click on the *Strong*'s reference number associated with our English word, it takes me to the *Strong*'s entry with the word in Hebrew or Greek, its pronunciation, part of speech and definition. It also lists all the other scriptures that use that same word, which often opens up a whole new path of study, because our English key words may never lead to the same scriptures as the original language.

Bible Promise Book

There are numerous Bible promise books that catalog the Bible's promises in any number of ways. In the front, there's usually a list of words you can scan, and when you find one that fits what you're looking for, you can go to the page that contains the list of scriptures on that topic.

Pastor, Bible Study Teacher or Learned Friend

Sometimes, when I don't know where to start or I want to know what others have learned on a particular topic, I'll ask my pastor, Bible study teacher or a trusted friend that I know studies the Bible and is familiar with what scripture says on a broad range of topics. Ask several! But again, take their answers and go to your own Bible to study the scriptures they reference.

The Entire Bible

Where studying a word in its original language is *a* favorite, this is *the* favorite approach I use. It is what I believe is the very best most comprehensive way to study a topic, but it is obviously time consuming and not always realistic for the quick counsel we often need for handling something God's way right now.

There are and have been a number times when I've gone to God desperate for Him to give me His truth and teaching on a subject directly from His word. Different conflicting "expert" interpretations can cause a lot of confusion as to what is the true meaning of God's word, and the bottom line is this: I don't want man's teaching; I want God to teach me.

When I use this approach, I first start with prayer, and I ask the Holy Spirit to teach me the Father's truth straight from the words of His mouth. I start in Genesis 1:1 and read the Bible from cover to cover with a specific focus on the question I have for God. The reason this is best is because not all of God's truth is categorized by a key word or phrase, and when I read His word from start to finish, He reveals things to me I otherwise never would have known or seen. And it allows me to see the entirety of His character and truth on a particular topic, not just a snapshot of a few verses.

Again, this is simply what I do. I hope it's helpful to you.

Let's Pray: Lord, we want to be taught by You as we study Your word. Inspire us and give us understanding as we seek to know You more and understand how to live for Your glory. Lead us to tools and people You wish to use to help us, but most of all, Holy Spirit, give us the desire and discipline to study Your word ourselves, testing everything we hear against the truth of scripture. Thank You, Lord, for Your word. Thank You that we have it in so many forms. Use it in us as You use us. In the sweet, holy and mighty name of Jesus, Amen.

Answer Key

Day 1: Let Love Be Without Hypocrisy

Practice & Prayer
1. His love for us
2. According to 2 Corinthians 5:14-15 –
    a. The love of Jesus
    b. Ourselves
    c. Jesus who died for us
    d. Answers will vary, but may sound something like this: if the love of Jesus compels us and we are living for Him, then we will choose to love others with warmth, kindness, and compassion because we love Jesus

Day 2: Abhor What Is Evil

Example
Ephesians 5:1-18 –
1. Fornication
2. Uncleanness
3. Covetousness
4. Filthiness
5. Foolish talking
6. Coarse jesting
7. Idolatry
8. Empty words
9. Disobedience
10. Foolish use of time
11. Drunkenness

Verse 11 – Unfruitful works of darkness
Verse 12 – In secret;
　　　　　Because they are shameful

Day 3: Cling to What Is Good

Teaching
First blank: Time
Second blank: Spend time with it
Third blank: God

Example
1. Peace
2. Justice, mercy, humility

3. Peace, edify
4. Love, spiritual gifts
5. Understanding, will, Lord
6. Yourselves, all
7. See list below:
    a. Righteousness
    b. Godliness
    c. Faith
    d. Love
    e. Patience
    f. Gentleness
8. Fight, faith, eternal life
9. Righteousness, faith, love, peace
10. Peace, holiness

Day 4: Be Kindly Affection with Brotherly Love

All answers will vary.

Day 5: Give Preference to One Another

Practice & Prayer
1. A living hope
2. An incorruptible, undefiled inheritance that does not fade away, reserved in heaven for us
3. We are kept by the power of God through faith for salvation to be revealed in the last time
4. For a little while, if need be, we might be grieved by various trials
5. For the testing of the genuineness of our faith
6. Much more precious than gold that parishes;
   Honor

Revelation 5:12 – the Lamb who was slain/Jesus

1 Peter 2:7 – precious

1 Peter 3:7 – as being heirs together of the grace of life

Day 6: Not Lagging in Diligence

Practice & Prayer

Scripture	Laziness	Diligence
Proverbs 10:4	poor	rich
Proverbs 12:24	put to forced labor	will rule
Proverbs 12:27	doesn't use his resources	precious possession
Proverbs 13:4	soul has unmet desires	soul is made rich
Proverbs 15:19	way is hedge of thorns	way is highway
Proverbs 19:15	suffers hunger	–
Proverbs 20:13	comes to poverty	satisfied with bread
Proverbs 21:5	–	plans lead to plenty
Proverbs 21:25	desire kills him; hands refuse to labor	–
Proverbs 26:16	wise in his own eyes	–
Ecclesiastes 10:18	building decays; house leaks	–

Day 7: Fervent in Spirit

Example
1. Instructed, way of the Lord
2. Spoke, taught
3. Boldly
4. Helped, believed
5. Refuted
6. Scriptures, Christ
7. Minister
8. Watered, seeds
9. What is written, puffed up, another
10. Unwilling, convenient

Day 8: Serving the Lord

Example
1. Fears
2. Sincerity, truth
3. Gods
4. Steward
5. Faithful
6. Mercies, kindness, humility, meekness, longsuffering;
7. Bears
8. Forgives
9. Love
10. Peace, rule
11. Thankful
12. Word, richly
13. Lord Jesus
14. Hardship, soldier
15. Quarrel
16. Gentle
17. Teach
18. Patient
19. Corrects

Day 9: Rejoicing in Hope

Example
1. Word
2. Happy
3. Scriptures
4. Spirit
5. Heaven
6. Gospel
7. Helmet
8. Firm, end
9. Anchor, sure, steadfast

Day 10: Patient in Tribulation

Example
1. Substance of things hoped for, evidence of things unseen
2. By faith
3. Answers will vary, but may include offer sacrifices, move with godly fear, inherit righteousness, obey, wait on God, receive strength, survive testing, believe God's promises, have courage, choose affliction over sin, esteem the reproach of Christ of greater riches than treasures, endure, receive protection and deliverance, subdue kingdoms, work righteousness, obtain promises, stop the mouths of lions, quench fire, escape the sword, are made strong, become valiant in battle, turn enemies to flight, receive the dead to life again, refuse deliverance from torture to obtain a better resurrection, endure physical torture and suffering, homelessness and poverty.
4. Without faith it is impossible to please God
5. Those who diligently seek Him
6. Answers may vary, but may say something like search out, seek, investigate, beg, crave, demand

Practice & Prayer
1. Abide in Christ
2. Answers may vary, but may say something like remain, not depart, to be held or kept continually, endure, wait for
3. Patience
4. By faith

Day 11: Continuing Steadfast in Prayer

All answers vary.

Day 12: Distributing to the Needs of the Saints

Practice & Prayer
Matthew 25:35-46 – Jesus
Acts 20:35 – It is more blessed to give than to receive
Philippians 2:1-4 – Selfish ambition;
                     In lowliness of mind, esteem others better than ourselves
Philippians 2:1-4 and Acts 20:35 – If we are selfish, we are thinking about what we can get. If we are esteeming others better than ourselves, we are focused on giving, and we will be the ones to be blessed
Philippians 2:4 and our life app – When we join together with other saints and become partners with them in what God is doing in their lives, we will be looking out for their interests

Day 13: Given to Hospitality

Example
Luke 19:5-6 – Joyful
Acts 28:7 – Courteous
Romans 16:2 – Worthy of the saints
Philippians 2:29 – Glad
1 Peter 4:9 – Without grumbling

3 John 1:5-8 – Faithful
Colossians 3:23-24 – Whatever we do, we should do heartily as unto the Lord and not to man, knowing our reward comes from Him alone
1 Thessalonians 5:16-18 –
1. Rejoice always
2. Pray without ceasing
3. In everything give thanks

Day 14: Bless Those Who Persecute You

Practice & Prayer
1. Afraid
2. Troubled
3. Sanctify
4. Defense
5. Meekness, fear
6. Conscience

What does the passage say will happen to those who confront us? They may be ashamed
What is the reason the passage gives us that Christ suffered for our sins? That He might bring us to God
What could happen when we suffer for the unjust? Jesus might bring them to God

Day 15: Bless and Do not Curse

Practice & Prayer
1. Sin, restrains
2. Wisdom, cut out
3. Piercings, wise, health
4. Preserves, destruction
5. Wise, fools
6. Wholesome, breaks
7. Sweetness, health
8. Spares, understanding, peace, perceptive
9. Guards, troubles
10. Hasty, fool

Day 16: Rejoice with Those Who Rejoice

Practice & Prayer
2. They came and held Him by the feet and worshiped Him
Reasons to rejoice:
  Deuteronomy 26:11 – for every good thing the LORD has given me and my family
  Psalms 5:11 – because our trust is in Him; because He defends us
  Psalms 13:5-6 – in His salvation; He has dealt bountifully with me
  Psalms 31:7 – because of His mercy; He considers my troubles; He knows my soul
  Psalms 63:7 – because He is my help; I am under the shadow of His wings
  Psalms 97:1 – because the LORD reigns
  Psalms 118:24 – because this is the day the LORD has made
  Joel 2:21 – He has done marvelous things
  Luke 6:23 – because our reward is great in heaven
  Luke 10:20 – because our names are written in heaven

John 16:22 – because we will see Jesus again; no one can take our joy

Acts 5:41 – when we are counted worthy to suffer shame for Jesus' name

Acts 11:23 – because we have seen the grace of God

Acts 15:30-31 – over the encouragement of God's word

Romans 5:2 – because we have access by faith into grace; have hope of the glory of God

Romans 5:11 – because through our Lord Jesus Christ, we have received the reconciliation

2 Corinthians 7:9 – for godly sorrow that leads to repentance

Philippians 1:18 – whether in pretense or truth, Christ is preached

Day 17: and Weep with Those Who Weep

Example
(verse 5) loved
(verse 7) go
(verse 23) hope
(verse 25) Him
(verse 26) believe
(verse 33) groaned, troubled
(verse 35) wept
(verse 36) loved

Day 18: Be of the Same Mind Toward One Another

Practice & Prayer
1. Spirit, Spirit
2. True, noble, just, pure, lovely, good report, virtue, praiseworthy
3. Above, mind

Day 19: Do not Set Your Minds on High Things

Practice & Prayer
Exodus 32:1 –delayed, gods, not know
Ezekiel 14:6 – repent, abominations
1 John 5:21 –keep

Day 20: but Associate with the Humble

Practice & Prayer
Matthew 7:13-14 – leads, leads
1 Peter 5:5 – submissive, humility;
            resists, proud, grace, humble
Matthew 11:29-30 – Jesus' yoke, easy, light, Jesus, gentle and lowly in heart

Day 21: Do not Be Wise in Your Own Opinion

Practice & Prayer
1. Trust, Lord, heart
2. Lean, understanding
3. All, acknowledge
4. Direct, paths

5. Wise, eyes
6. Fear, Lord
7. Depart, evil

Verse 8 – health, flesh, strength, bones
Psalm 119:105 – word, lamp, light
Proverbs 16:20 – heeds, good, happy
Proverbs 28:25-26 –proud, strife, trusts, prospered, own, fool, wisely, delivered

Day 22: Repay No One Evil for Evil

Practice & Prayer
 1 Peter 3:8-11 –
  verse 8: one mind, compassion, Love, tenderhearted, courteous
  verse 9: evil, blessing
  verse 10: tongue, lips
  verse 11: evil, good, peace
 Verse 12 –
  Do good: eyes, righteous, open, prayers
  Do evil: face, against
 Verse 15 – sanctify
    always, defense, hope
 Verse 17 – better, will, good, evil

Day 23: Have Regard for Good Things in the Sight of All Men

Practice & Prayer
1. Verse 6 – cast out, withered, fire, burned
2. Verse 7 – abide, words, desire, done
3. Verses 8-9 – glorified, fruit, disciples, loved, loved
4. Verse 10 – commandments, love, I, abide

Day 24: If It Is Possible, as Much as It Depends on You, Live Peaceably with All Men

All answers will vary.

Day 25: Beloved, Do not Avenge Yourselves

Practice & Prayer
Ten Keys to Trusting Our True Avenger
1. Lift, soul
2. Trust, God
3. Ashamed
4. Enemies, triumph
5. Wait, ashamed
6. Cause
7. Show, ways, teach, paths
8. Lead, truth
9. God , salvation
10. Wait, day

Day 26: Give Place to Wrath

Practice & Prayer
Psalm 37:34 –
Keep, way
Exalt, wicked, see
Proverbs 17:5 –
Calamity, unpunished
Proverbs 24:17-18 –
Rejoice, falls, heart, glad, stumbles, displease, away

Day 27: Give Your Enemy Food and Drink

Practice & Prayer
Exodus 23:4-5 – enemy's, astray, hates, refrain, help
1 Thessalonians 5:15 – yourselves, all

Day 28: Heap Coals of Fire on the Enemy's Head

Practice & Prayer
Romans 2:4 – goodness
Ephesians 2:8 – grace, gift
charis – kindness, influence, Christ, exercise

Day 29: Do not Be Overcome by Evil

Practice & Prayer
Ephesians 6:11-20 –
Verse 11: the whole armor of God; that you may be able to stand against the schemes of the devil
Verse 12: flesh, blood, principalities, powers, rulers, darkness, spiritual hosts, wickedness, heavenly
Verse 13: Therefore take up the whole armor of God; withstand in the evil day
Verses 14-18 –
Verse 14: truth, the breastplate of righteousness
Verse 15: the gospel of peace
Verse 16: the shield of faith; quench the fiery darts of the wicked one
Verse 17: helmet of salvation; sword of the Spirit; the word of God
Verse 18: praying always with all prayer and supplication in the Spirit
Verse 19: being watchful to the end with all perseverance and supplication for all saints
How might we put on this armor every day?
Answers will vary, but might include spend time in the word, which is truth. Do what God tells us to do, which secures the breastplate of righteousness. Be prepared to share the gospel with those God puts in our path, living at peace with all men as much as it is possible. Recall and remind ourselves of who God says He is and what He says He'll do. This is declaring truth as well as strengthening our faith. Preach the gospel to ourselves, reminding ourselves that we are saved by grace through faith and nothing else, using knowledge and acknowledgement to secure the helmet of salvation on our heads. Respond to the devil's temptations and attacks with the word of God, just like Jesus did, wielding our sword. Pray every day, in the Spirit, for ourselves and all the saints.
Verses 19-20 – utterance, boldly, gospel, chains, boldly

216

Day 30: Overcome Evil with Good

Practice & Prayer

Why do you think the Holy Spirit is key to our walking the talk?

(Answers will vary. Because there is nothing good in our flesh, if we're doing anything by our own power or might, it's not going to go well. We don't have the power to accomplish God's will; it has to be by His power. It's not in us to walk His walk unless He is walking it out in us.)

Ephesians 3:14-16 – to be strengthened with might through His Spirit in the inner man

Ephesians 3:20-21 – according to the power that works in us

Philippians 1:19 – the supply of the Spirit of Jesus Christ

2 Peter 1:3 – by His divine power

Romans 8:1 – there is now no condemnation

       – walk, flesh, Spirit

Twelve Truths About Walking by the Spirit

1. Things, Spirit
2. Life, peace
3. Flesh, please
4. Dead, life, righteousness
5. Spirit
6. Lust, flesh
7. Led
8. Recognize, works
9. Spirit, fruit
10. Bondage
11. Sufferings
12. Crucified, Spirit

Jude 1:20-21 –

1. Build yourselves up on your most holy faith
2. Pray in the Holy Spirit
3. Keep yourselves in the love of God
4. Look for the mercy of our Lord Jesus Christ unto eternal life

2 Timothy 3:5 – having a form of godliness but denying its power

www.ingramcontent.com/pod-product-compliance
Lightning Source LLC
Chambersburg PA
CBHW050013110426

42741CB00038B/3386